T0195615

THE GREATEST

CHRISTIAN LACHANCE

WESTBOW
PRESS®
A DIVISION OF THOMAS NELSON
& ZONDERVAN

The Authorized (King James) Version of the Bible ('the KJV'), the rights in which are vested in the Crown in the United Kingdom, is reproduced here by permission of the Crown's patentee, Cambridge University Press.

This book is a work of non-fiction. Unless otherwise noted, the author and the publisher make no explicit guarantees as to the accuracy of the information contained in this book and in some cases, names of people and places have been altered to protect their privacy.

WestBow Press books may be ordered through booksellers or by contacting:

WestBow Press
A Division of Thomas Nelson & Zondervan
1663 Liberty Drive
Bloomington, IN 47403
www.westbowpress.com
1 (866) 928-1240

Because of the dynamic nature of the Internet, any web addresses or links contained in this book may have changed since publication and may no longer be valid. The views expressed in this work are solely those of the author and do not necessarily reflect the views of the publisher, and the publisher hereby disclaims any responsibility for them.

Any people depicted in stock imagery provided by Getty Images are models, and such images are being used for illustrative purposes only. Certain stock imagery © Getty Images.

ISBN: 978-1-9736-2395-3 (sc)
ISBN: 978-1-9736-2397-7 (hc)
ISBN: 978-1-9736-2396-0 (e)

Library of Congress Control Number: 2018903698

Print information available on the last page.

WestBow Press rev. date: 4/3/2018

To my Lord and Savior, Jesus Christ, who walked
with me through good times and bad

To my wonderful son, Noah, may you always
remember how much God loves you

To my friend, June, you are a blessing beyond measure.
Thank you for your help and encouragement.

FINDING THE GREATEST JOY

Within all of us is the desire to find true happiness. This desire is so great that it's even written in our US Constitution that we have the right to pursue happiness.

Happiness comes and goes with our circumstances, but joy lasts forever. The key is to find real joy—a joy that can fill your heart despite the trials and testing you may be facing. That is the greatest joy—a joy that cannot be taken away from you.

Over the years, God has done a miracle with me. He has truly changed my life. And not just that, he's also altered how I see things. He has given me a new hope and filled my heart with real joy. Everything I know, he has taught me. Through every struggle I faced, he has brought me wisdom and changed my heart for the better. God has guided me through the toughest of times and taught me many lessons.

It has not been an easy path. But I would gladly walk this path again if it means I could bring hope to someone else. Through reading his Word, I have been given strength and peace. God has brought me to where I am now—a place of healing, faith, and everlasting joy.

Now it is my pleasure to share what I've learned with others. May God bless you and encourage you with the words he has given me.

JOY

You may have heard the word *joy* used as an acronym.

J—Jesus

O—Others

Y—Yourself

When we put things in that order, we are given more strength, love, and joy in our lives from God, our almighty Father.

J—Jesus

Jesus must come first. He is the only one who can save our souls from eternal separation from God. He draws us near with his love and gives us all the support we need in this life. It takes a personal faith and trust in him and him alone to get to heaven.

The following devotions tell about Jesus and the great God and Creator we have. My hope is that each devotion will help you know him more.

A LIGHT THAT SHINES
FOREVER MORE

The first snowstorm of the year hit. It came as a surprise to us, as it was sixty degrees a few days earlier. We were blessed that we didn't lose power with all the ice. I remember years back when many people lost power for weeks at a time. They struggled to survive the winter storms.

When storms come, the power may be knocked out, but we are not completely in darkness. We have a light that shines throughout the world. That light is Jesus. He outshines poverty, hunger, grief and sadness, and depression and anger that reside in our hearts. And he victoriously outshines sin. That's why he came to this earth as a helpless baby so many years ago. He came to be born as our Savior. He came to die for you and me.

Death had no victory over him. He defeated death when he rose again three days later. He defeated sin and the troubles of this world. He continues to defeat these things for us today when we invite him into our hearts and accept him as our Savior.

Won't you invite him into your heart? He will forever be your victorious shining light.

"For thou wilt light my candle: the Lord my God will enlighten my darkness" (Psalm 18:28).

"O death, where is thy sting? O grave, where is thy victory? The sting of death is sin; and the strength of sin is the law. But thanks be to God, which giveth us the victory through our Lord Jesus Christ" (1 Corinthians 15:55–57).

"Then spake Jesus again unto them, saying, I am the light of the world: he that followeth me shall not walk in darkness, but shall have the light of life" (John 8:12).

"Let your light so shine before men, that they may see your good works, and glorify your Father which is in heaven" (Matthew 5:16).

A NEW YEAR, A NEW PATH

The beginning of the New Year is like standing at the foot of a path. You pause at the edge, wondering what twists, bends, and hills you will face. You may have new goals you want to achieve. You may meet new people and add them to your circle of friends. A new home or a change of career might be in store for you. Perhaps new life will be added to your family with the birth of a baby.

For some people, this year will bring a much-needed second chance at a new beginning. It's out with the old year and in with the new as you look forward to what's ahead. A new year is always a precious gift from God, for it is another year to live for him.

In the beginning, you will start out strong and confident, but when the path gets tough, you may get down. Be sure to keep your head up and keep going. Yes, you may fall at times and feel discouraged, but there is hope. You can find your way to the end. You never have to travel this path alone. A hand is always reaching down to pick you up.

You have a loving Savior and God. Jesus will provide for you. He will always give you what you need to endure until the end. Don't be afraid to let go and let him completely take over and carry you. It will be his pleasure to do so. He will protect you and comfort you in times of need and lift you up. Even when things are going great, he is there by your side to share in your joy.

And as you journey down this path of a new year together, God will be sure to invite friends and family to stand along the side to cheer you on and pray for you all the way.

"Thy word is a lamp unto my feet, and a light unto my path" (Psalm 119:105).

"The Lord is my strength and my shield; my heart trusted in him, and I am helped: therefore my heart greatly rejoiceth; and with my song will I praise him" (Psalm 28:7).

"He restoreth my soul: he leadeth me in the paths of righteousness for his name's sake" (Psalm 23:3).

"Trust in the Lord with all thine heart; and lean not unto thine own understanding. In all thy ways acknowledge him, and he shall direct thy paths" (Proverbs 3:5–6).

ACCORDING TO PLAN

We all make plans of some sort. Having a plan can be a good thing. Some people can't function without a plan or a to-do list in place. When things don't go according to plan, such people get frustrated and stressed out. In the end, things eventually fall into place and often turn out better than these people originally intended. A good plan takes time and patience.

God has the best plans of all of us. His plans are always perfect. We may not see what he's doing at first, but we can trust he has our best interests in mind.

Exodus 1–14 tells the story of Moses, who lived a life that was according to God's plan. He was born a Hebrew, and at that time, the Hebrews were slaves to the Egyptians. Pharaoh had commanded that all Hebrew babies be cast into the river. Moses's life was in danger, but God saved him. His mother hid him for three months and then laid him in a basket near the edge of the river. Pharaoh's own daughter found and adopted him. He grew up living the life of luxury, being raised as an Egyptian in Pharaoh's house.

One day when he was grown up, he killed an Egyptian who was smiting a Hebrew slave. You might be thinking, *What a shame. He threw it all away after that preparation for leadership.* But God had a plan for Moses.

Moses feared that what he had done would be known to everyone, so he fled to the land of Midian. There he got married, had two sons, and became a shepherd. It might sound like his life turned out good after all, but God still had something far better for Moses.

God's thoughts are not our thoughts (Isa. 55:8). God sees what we can't see, and he knows the future. He also knows what's best for everyone. God was planning on helping not just Moses but all the Hebrew people.

God called Moses to serve a greater purpose. He told Moses to go back to Egypt and lead his precious nation of Israel out of slavery to the land they were promised. It wouldn't be easy. Moses would have to face his fears as well as stand against Pharaoh. The task was great. He would have to lead over six hundred thousand men, plus the women and children. Moses knew no one would believe him. I bet you're thinking it would have been better for him to stay a shepherd!

When God calls us to do something, we may not understand it. It may seem impossible at first, but he always gives us the strength, the support, and the guidance we need to be successful. God provided Aaron, Moses's brother, to speak for Moses. God brought the plagues that were needed to convince Pharaoh to let God's people go. God even parted the Red Sea so the Israelites could walk through safely to the other side. In the end, Moses led the Hebrew people to freedom with God's help.

God's plan for us is greater than we could ever imagine. His thoughts are higher than our thoughts. His ways are greater than ours. His purpose for us has more meaning. There isn't anyone he couldn't use to do great things. He has a plan for each of us. And don't forget the best part. The life he has for us in eternity is far better than what we hang on to here in this world. Do you know God's amazing plan for you?

"For my thoughts are not your thoughts, neither are your ways my ways, saith the LORD" (Isaiah 55:8).

"For I know the thoughts that I think toward you, saith the LORD, thoughts of peace, and not of evil, to give you an expected end" (Jeremiah 29:11).

"Search me, O God, and know my heart: try me, and know my thoughts: And see if there be any wicked way in me, and lead me in the way everlasting" (Psalm 139:23–24).

"And we know that all things work together for good to them that love God, to them who are the called according to his purpose" (Romans 8:28).

ATTENTION TO DETAIL

Sitting at Fork Stark in New Castle, New Hampshire, I looked out at the glistening blue water stretching to the mouth of the Piscataqua River. A lighthouse sat on an island all its very own. A boat passed by, making ripples in the otherwise calm river, as it slowly moved with the current.

Birds of yellow, white, brown, and black flew over the river and across the land, looking for their next meal. Dark rocks covered in seaweed added a rich color standing out against the light blue water. Tall trees covered with green leaves reached up to the blue sky and fluffy white clouds. The lush green grass sprinkled with purple and yellow flowers added the perfect touch to the scene.

Until now, one of my favorite places to visit was the beach, but for some reason, this place seemed so much more beautiful. It must have had something to do with all its details. The blue ocean against its equally blue sky is wonderful to see, but when you compare it to the flowers, grass, and rocks this place has to offer, it stands out so much more.

God has done an amazing job adding so much detail to the stunning world around us. All we have to do is stop and see it. Just take it all in and notice every piece he so carefully puts in place.

Our lives are like that too. He paints a magnificent portrait with each detail in our life, from the home we live in to the family and friends he brings to us and the career he calls us to. He places in our lives exactly what needs to be there, good and bad. The good shows the abundant blessings he wants to give us. The bad helps us grow in faith and trust in him. Each detail in our lives makes his awesome strength and love stand out more.

If our lives were plain and simple, they would be nothing more than a blue sky against a blue ocean. Our God is a much more creative artist than that.

"And God called the dry land Earth; and the gathering together of the waters called he Seas: and God saw that it was good" (Genesis 1:10).

"The fowl of the air, and the fish of the sea, and whatsoever passeth through the paths of the seas. O LORD our Lord, how excellent is thy name in all the earth!" (Psalm 8:8–9).

"Behold the fowls of the air: for they sow not, neither do they reap, nor gather into barns; yet your heavenly Father feedeth them. Are ye not much better than they?" (Matthew 6:26).

"The LORD on high is mightier than the noise of many waters, yea, than the mighty waves of the sea" (Psalm 93:3).

FROM AMONG THE THORNS

Out from amongst the thorns comes a beautiful rose. Can something good come from something bad?

Yes, I have seen God make good things come out of a bad situation. The flooding of a church is used to help its church members band together and strengthen their communication. A person getting injured is used to bring sympathy to others as well as bring friends and loved ones to church.

How about the sufferings that Jesus went through? All that he endured was used to bring hope and healing to others through his precious gift of salvation. If the blind were never blind, then we couldn't read how he healed them. If the sick didn't suffer physically, then they wouldn't have known the miracle of God's healing power through his precious Son.

Even in my own life, I see that, if I didn't go through the loss of my mom, then I wouldn't have the understanding and care to be there for others who are going through the same heartache. If I didn't struggle financially, I wouldn't be trusting God to provide for my needs. Neither would I be able to experience all the blessings and miracles he gave me. I wouldn't have the close and personal relationship that I have with him now.

God is forever faithful to those who seek him in trials and tribulations. He never leaves us nor forsakes us. He takes the trying times we go through and uses them to mold us, strengthen our character, and help us see his mighty hand at work.

As you go through your own heartache, sickness, and trying times, turn them over to God and ask for the strength you need to wait patiently for him to work. For in the end, God will show you something wonderful that could only come from being among the thorns.

"He answered and said, Lo, I see four men loose, walking in the midst of the fire, and they have no hurt; and the form of the fourth is like the Son of God" (Daniel 3:25).

"And not only so, but we glory in tribulations also: knowing that tribulation worketh patience; And patience, experience; and experience, hope" (Rom. 5:3–4).

"The steps of a good man are ordered by the LORD: and he delighteth in his way. Though he fall, he shall not be utterly cast down: for the LORD upholdeth him with his hand. I have been young, and now am old; yet have I not seen the righteous forsaken, nor his seed begging bread" (Ps. 37:23–25).

GOD IS ALWAYS THERE

The message on the daily calendar read "ASAP: Always Say a Prayer." That message couldn't have come at a better time. I was feeling burdened by the sicknesses and hardships of those around me. That message reminded me that, when bad things are going on in my life or in the life of those close to me, I was to always stop and turn to God for help.

Whether we are facing problems in our own life or hearing about them in someone else's, we can become depressed and feel helpless. It becomes harder to focus on our normal everyday tasks. Before you know it, the problems start to have an impact on every area of our life. As we try to wait patiently for an answer to prayer or a glimmer of hope, we get impatient and take our focus off turning to God for help and start to look for a solution ourselves. Then the harder we try to hang on, the more we lose our grip.

It's like the time the apostles saw Jesus walking on the water during a storm. Peter was so focused on Jesus that he was willing to jump out of the boat to get closer to him. When he noticed how strong the wind was around him, he took his eyes off Jesus and began to sink in the waves. When Jesus stretched forth his hand to save Peter, he said to him, "Oh thou of little faith, wherefore didst thou doubt" (Matt. 14:31).

We may feel like God is only with us when life is going good. Then the moment something bad happens, we feel like he has abandoned us, and we don't know why. During those times, we need to remember the promise he gave us in his Word, "I will never leave thee, nor forsake thee" (Heb. 13:5).

God is always just one prayer away. All we need to do is reach out to God and draw closer to him. When the waves get rough and trouble is all around us, we know we will be safe if we keep our eyes focused on him. Always remember, no matter what's going on around us, God is always there, and he will endure with us until the end.

"And when the disciples saw him walking on the sea, they were troubled, saying, It is a spirit; and they cried out for fear. But straightway Jesus spake unto them, saying, Be of good cheer; it is I; be not afraid" (Matthew 14:26–27).

"Be still, and know that I am God: I will be exalted among the heathen, I will be exalted in the earth" (Psalm 46:10).

"Have not I commanded thee? Be strong and of a good courage; be not afraid, neither be thou dismayed: for the Lord thy God is with thee whithersoever thou goest" (Joshua 1:9).

"Draw nigh to God, and he will draw nigh to you" (James 4:8).

GOD'S HAND IN IT ALL

The strong crashing waves smooth the rocks on the beach. The pressure of the earth brings forth a diamond out of coal. Did you ever stop to think the problems you face in life may not be a sign that God doesn't love you, but that he loves you enough to polish you and work on you so you will one day shine like gold?

God may not prevent the storm that you are going through from happening, but he will use it to strengthen you and draw you close to him. If everything were perfect in life and all things went according to plan, would you feel you needed God? Perhaps not. Would you feel a great desire to look forward to your home in heaven? God knows our needs more than we do. He knows we need to grow in faith. A rose bush cannot bloom with beautiful flowers without first being pruned.

In the midst of the storm, God will not leave you comfortless. He will hold you up and strengthen your faith as you cling to him among the breaking waves. He is forever faithful to keep a watchful eye on us, and as a loving father, he will reach his hands down and draw us ever closer to him.

To God be the glory and power forever, for only he can get us through the trials we face and on to the green paths of the many blessings ahead of us.

"*Teaching them to observe all things whatsoever I have commanded you: and, lo, I am with you alway, even unto the end of the world. Amen*" (Matthew 28:20).

"*And he arose, and rebuked the wind, and said unto the sea, Peace, be still. And the wind ceased, and there was a great calm*" (Mark 4:39).

"*God is our refuge and strength, a very present help in trouble*" (Psalm 46:1).

"*I will not leave you comfortless: I will come to you. Yet a little while, and the world seeth me no more; but ye see me: because I live, ye shall live also*" (John 14:17–19).

GOD'S UNCONDITIONAL LOVE

If you read in the book of Jeremiah, it's touching to see the way God loves Israel. Jeremiah goes into detail about Israel's disobedience and how God allowed them to be taken into captivity. They were following false prophets and failed to change their ways. But even though they were disobedient, God still loved them and gave them hope for the future. He promised to bring them out of captivity and be their God and love them. He still promises that to them for all eternity when Jesus returns someday.

Imagine, God still loved his people even after they did all that. So let's think about how much he loves us and how much he wants to bless us in our lives and rescue us from the captivity of this world. He wants to provide for all our needs and keep us close to him.

The best news is that nothing is too hard for him. I mean *nothing*. And to prove it, he gives us his word. Twice, God reminds his people in Jeremiah 32 that nothing is too hard for him.

If that's not enough, remember the story of Abraham and Sarah at the golden age of one hundred and ninety. Sarah was way beyond childbearing age, and still God reminded them that nothing was too hard for him. So he gave them a son, Isaac, and from Abraham's seed created the nation of Israel. That's our God, the God of possibilities because he loves us unconditionally and nothing is beyond his control.

"But God, who is rich in mercy, for his great love wherewith he loved us, Even when we were dead in sins, hath quickened us together with Christ, (by grace ye are saved;)" (Ephesians 2:4–5).

"Ah Lord God! behold, thou hast made the heaven and the earth by thy great power and stretched out arm, and there is nothing too hard for thee" (Jeremiah 32:17).

"Behold, I am the LORD, the God of all flesh: is there any thing too hard for me?" (Jeremiah 32:27).

"Is any thing too hard for the LORD? At the time appointed I will return unto thee, according to the time of life, and Sarah shall have a son" (Genesis 18:14).

LESS IS MORE

God uses what we have and makes it to be more than what it is. Last week I was so worried about having enough food that I stocked up more than usual. I even went over budget. There was just enough for the week. This past week, I spent less money and bought less food, but somehow there still was more than enough to last all week.

Whenever I have less of something, God somehow multiplies it and makes it last longer. When I have less time, money, and food, I learn to put my full faith and trust in God to provide for me. When I do that, he rewards me by supplying for all my needs.

In the Old Testament, Elijah, one of God's prophets, visited a poor widow while there was a famine in the land.[1] He asked her to give him some water and something to eat. She sadly told him that she only had enough food for one meal, which she was going to make for her and her son to eat before they died. He reassured her that her supply would last, but to make him a little cake first. She obeyed despite the fact that he was a stranger to her.

Would you believe that each day as she scraped the barrel of meal and poured out the cruse of oil that there was always enough for another meal for all three of them? God made it so they would eat for another day and another day after that. They had enough food to last until the rain came down again.

God always provides for us in our greatest time of need. We only need to trust him. What are you running out of: food, money, or strength? Surrender what little you have to the Lord. He will always multiply it abundantly.

---

[1] Elijah and the widow's story taken from 1 Kings 17:10–16.

"For thus saith the LORD God of Israel, The barrel of meal shall not waste, neither shall the cruse of oil fail, until the day that the LORD sendeth rain upon the earth. And she went and did according to the saying of Elijah: and she, and he, and her house, did eat many days" (1 Kings 17:14–15).

"And there was nothing lacking to them, neither small nor great, neither sons nor daughters, neither spoil, nor any thing that they had taken to them: David recovered all" (1 Samuel 30:19).

"But my God shall supply all your need according to his riches in glory by Christ Jesus" (Philippians 4:19).

LITTLE BLESSINGS, BIG RAINFALL

Rain can put a damper on any camping trip. This is what my son and I went through this past summer. I sat in my car fuming, praying, and shouting some not so nice words toward God in my head as I watched the rain come down on our tent site. Needless to say, yes, I was very upset with the rain. I was so looking forward to this camping trip and much needed vacation with my son. God's silence when I prayed he would take away the rain made it worse. Even when it seems like he isn't listening, he is still working.

The rain might have been falling, but a silver lining was still in the clouds. My eighteen-year-old son was more an adult about things than I was that day. He was still excited and working on trying to build a fire despite all the wetness. He put things into perspective when he pointed out that we were away camping and others were going through a lot worse than a little rain.

After a while, we decided to take a ride and go get some pizza at a favorite pizza place that we visited every year on our trip. So there we were, enjoying dinner, watching highlights from the Olympics, and having things turn out for the best.

The rain stopped for a while when we were done. When it started up again, we climbed in the tent and shared some laughs over a card game. Suddenly we saw a yellowish bright light flashing outside the tent. We looked at each other in amazement and went outside. The fire my son was trying to start miraculously flared up on its own! God started our fire for us. The rain slowed down to a few drops so we could enjoy the time around the glow of the fire.

It rained all night while we slept, but inside the tent, we were warm and dry. Sunshine greeted us the next morning, and the blessings began to flow. Oh, what a day we had swimming in the crystal clear pond that was so warm that it was like bathwater. We cooked the leftover pizza and garlic bread on the metal grill over the fire as an experiment, and it turned out to be a delightful treat. For dessert, we stuffed ice cream cones with marshmallows, chocolate, and strawberries, rolled them in tin foil, and put them on the fire. S'mores with style!

We even made a new friend. A little chipmunk we called Chippy often came out of his hole to greet us. He really added to our entertainment that afternoon.

If it weren't for the rain the day before, we wouldn't have enjoyed our camping experience all the more so. I enjoyed watching my son come alive as he took care of the fire, fed the chipmunk, and really embraced the outdoor life.

The rain brought a humbling spirit in me with the realization that there is a bigger picture out there than just what's in my life. I pictured a farmer not so far away thanking God for the rain for his crops. The rain enhanced the colors of the woods and the sweet smell of the plants, another reminder of its importance, to feed all the wildlife and flora around us.

You can be sure at the end of our blessed day that I took out my Bible and began to read and pray for God's forgiveness as well as praise him for the rain.

"Call unto me, and I will answer thee, and shew thee great and mighty things, which thou knowest not" (Jeremiah 33:3).

"Ask ye of the LORD rain in the time of the latter rain; so the LORD shall make bright clouds, and give them showers of rain, to every one grass in the field" (Zechariah 10:1).

"For the earth which drinketh in the rain that cometh oft upon it, and bringeth forth herbs meet for them by whom it is dressed, receiveth blessing from God" (Hebrews 6:7).

"And all these blessings shall come on thee, and overtake thee, if thou shalt hearken unto the voice of the LORD thy God" (Deuteronomy 28:2).

LOOK FOR THE POSITIVES

My mom always encouraged me to count my blessings. This wasn't always easy for me. I'll admit I haven't always been a "glass is half full" type of person. It's easier to focus on the negative things in any situation. It is harder to see the positive side. Even though my mom was a single mom with two kids, she would say that things could always be worse. She would look for ways to be grateful. One of her most famous lines was, "I am grateful my children are healthy and I'm not driving to Boston's Children's Hospital to visit one of them."

When I see wives getting frustrated and angry with their husbands, I want to tell them, "Picture yourself waking up Christmas morning. The house is quiet, the kids are gone with their dad, and you're all alone." There were many Christmases when my mom would have been grateful to have someone to be frustrated with.

Sometimes we don't realize what we have until we see what's missing in someone else's life. The secret to being positive is to stop and see that you have more in life than you realize.

There have been times when I have really struggled financially as a single mom, but when I stop and think of the moms in Uganda who have to work morning to night just to feed their children one meal a day and live in a leaky shack, I realize how much God has blessed me.

Whenever I get frustrated with my son, I stop for a moment and thank God that I have him in my life. I thank God for the opportunity to be a mom. I think of how my son has grown and all he has accomplished.

When Paul and Silas were in prison in the book of Acts, they were beaten, chained, and thrown into nothing more than a hole in the ground. But even when they were in the most horrible situation, they sang hymns and praises at midnight.

They saw the positives. They knew that, even though they had nothing else in life, they still had an amazingly powerful God who was in control and who loved them so much that he caused an earthquake to break the chains and set them free.

There is nothing too hard for our God. There is nothing he can't provide in order to meet our needs. Sometimes he wants us to stop and see what we already have before he gives us more. He wants us to learn how to look for the positives.

"And at midnight Paul and Silas prayed, and sang praises unto God: and the prisoners heard them" (Acts 16:25).

"Finally, brethren, whatsoever things are true, whatsoever things are honest, whatsoever things are just, whatsoever things are pure, whatsoever things are lovely, whatsoever things are of good report; if there be any virtue, and if there be any praise, think on these things" (Philippians 4:8).

"Not that I speak in respect of want: for I have learned, in whatsoever state I am, therewith to be content" (Philippians 4:11).

MY GOD

Over the years, there have been times when I didn't have enough money to pay my rent or buy food. After a brief moment of panic, I would stop and pray and ask God for help. Before you know it, a miracle would take place. An unexpected check would come in the mail. A friend would feel led to give me the exact amount of money I needed. God would have money come from the most unexpected place or people. During times like these, God truly reminded me of who is.

You see, I know that my God is the same God who parted the Red Sea one day for his people to walk safely on dry land. He is the same God who fed more than five thousand in one sitting with just five loaves of bread and two fish (Matt. 14:15–21). This is the same God who continues to provide for my family and me every day.

My God is the same God who created the earth and the heavens above. He created so much beauty in this world to enjoy. Every beautiful sunset I see reflects only a spark of his great love for us. Oh, how I love to watch the sunsets when I am having such a rough day. I sit in awe as I think about all that God has done for me. I think about all the hard times he has helped me overcome.

I know that my God is also the same God that gave the first Christmas gift to all the world. He gave his only Son Jesus as a sacrifice for our sins. The only way I could possibly try to thank him for all he is and all he has done is to give him my life.

My God is the same God who will always be faithful and true. After all he has done in our lives, he waits patiently with his arms stretched out, saying, "Come unto me and I will give you rest." He reassures us to keep up the faith and to trust him because he will always be there for us.

When all seemed lost, I know it was my God that got me through.

"Casting all your care upon him; for he careth for you" (2 Peter 5:7).

"If ye then, being evil, know how to give good gifts unto your children, how much more shall your Father which is in heaven give good things to them that ask him?" (Matthew 7:11).

"And also that every man should eat and drink, and enjoy the good of all his labour, it is the gift of God" (Ecclesiastes 3:13).

"Every good gift and every perfect gift is from above, and cometh down from the Father of lights, with whom is no variableness, neither shadow of turning" (James 1:17).

MY INNER STRENGTH AND COURAGE

On the drive home from the doctor's today, I just wasn't feeling well at all. I happened to look up and see a little bird trying so hard to attack a large crow. The little bird was right on top of him. I have to say it fought quite valiantly and the crow just kept trying to get away. I can only assume that the crow was going after the little bird's nest or food. I was amazed that the little bird had no fear. It had such determination. It didn't give up. I admired the strength and courage that little bird had.

I pictured that big black crow being a symbol of the challenges and hardships we face in life. I thought to myself, *I would like to be like that little bird and have the same courage and determination to overcome whatever trials life put in my way.*

A Bible verse instantly came to mind. "Where there is no vision the people perish" (Prov. 29:18). We need a vision or something to focus our eyes on, to keep us going. For the little bird, it was the sense to protect whatever the crow was going after. Once we have that vision, if we surrender it to Jesus and ask for him to provide the strength we need, he will give us that strength and courage to face any battles in our way.

David was a lowly shepherd boy who knew Israel was under the threat of the Philistines. Like that little bird, he didn't care about his size. He had a vision to save Israel. He drew his courage and strength from God, his Savior, and defeated the mighty giant Goliath with a slingshot and a stone.

Don't get discouraged when the black crows come at you. Keep your vision in mind. Draw your strength and courage from Jesus, our Almighty God.

From the book of Chronicles, when Israel was under the threat of attack from the Assyrians, I love the response King Hezekiah had for them. "Be strong and courageous, be not afraid nor dismayed for the king of Assyria, nor for all the multitude that is with him: for there be more with us than with him: With him is an arm of flesh; but with us is the LORD our God to help us, and to fight our battles" (2 Chron. 32:8–9).

"Where there is no vision, the people perish: but he that keepeth the law happy is he" (Proverbs 29:18).

"David said moreover, The LORD that delivered me out of the paw of the lion, and out of the paw of the bear, he will deliver me out of the hand of this Philistine. And Saul said unto David, Go, and the LORD be with thee" (1 Samuel 17:37).

"Then said David to the Philistine, Thou comest to me with a sword, and with a spear, and with a shield: but I come to thee in the name of the LORD of hosts, the God of the armies of Israel, whom thou hast defied" (1 Samuel 17:45).

OUR HELP IN TIME OF NEED

No matter how big or small, God cares about it all. Can you imagine the Almighty Creator of the heavens and earth takes the time to help us with the little troubles we have to face day to day?

He formed the thundering, lava-filled volcanoes. His hand is on the waves of the mighty uncontrollable seas. Yet in my day when I struggle with a task or can't find my keys, he takes the time to help me, no matter how great or small the need.

Our God has more to do than every human who has ever lived on the earth put together. Despite how much he holds in his hands, like a good heavenly Father, he is always able to make our individual needs his number-one priority.

I experienced his hand upon me one day as I had a moment of insanity in the parking lot at Fox Run Crossings shopping center. I came out of Kohl's and was positive that I parked my car in front of Staples. So I headed that way. I was so sure of where my car was, but after walking around the rows of cars for twenty minutes, I started to get confused. I couldn't find my car. I broke down in tears. A few people tried to help me, while others passed by without even looking in my direction.

I called a friend and asked her to pray for me. She was so caring and understanding. Then I prayed and asked God to please help me find my car. Even though I panicked at first and thought it was stolen, a great calming sense of peace came over me. The tears might have flowed, but my heart felt God's grace and assurance that it was going to be all right.

Finally one of the store managers was kind enough to walk through the parking lot with me. God led us right to my car, and it was safe and sound. I completely forgot that I moved my car before going into another store. It had been a long, hard week, and I was having trouble remembering things.

As I think back, I can't help but wonder how many people watching me wander around aimlessly paused for a moment in their day and prayed for me. It's a comfort to know God's hand was upon me and all those who experienced this with me.

There's never a problem too big for God to handle—nor too small for him to care about—when it comes to the needs of his precious children. He will always help us in our time of need.

"I will lift up mine eyes unto the hills, from whence cometh my help. My help cometh from the LORD, which made heaven and earth" (Psalm 121:1).

"The LORD shall preserve thee from all evil: he shall preserve thy soul. The LORD shall preserve thy going out and thy coming in from this time forth, and even for evermore" (Psalm 121:7–8).

"God is in the midst of her; she shall not be moved: God shall help her, and that right early" (Psalm 46:5).

"The name of the LORD is a strong tower: the righteous runneth into it, and is safe" (Proverbs 18:10).

PASSING THE TEST

Does anyone really like to take tests? I know some people get severe test anxiety. There are many types of tests: academic, medical, work related, and so on. No matter what type of test it is, no one really enjoys taking them. There's usually stress, anxiety, worry, and sometimes a lot of emotional buildup and preparation involved beforehand.

God has his own type of testing. One of his most famous tests was when he tested Abraham and asked him to sacrifice his son, Isaac.[2] Abraham passed with grace and ease. How did he pass God's testing? With faith and trust. Abraham had a strong faith in God and trusted that God knew what he was doing.

Over the years, I have been through many tests from God. Some I passed; unfortunately, others I didn't. It's hard to see what God may be doing behind the scenes in our lives. He may be testing our faith and belief in him, or he might be working on our hearts and molding us in order to prepare us for what's coming in our future.

In my life, not only has he tested my faith, he's also tested my obedience to him. That's something he is working with me on right now. When finances seem rocky or an opportunity comes along for a career change, I have this inner feeling that tells me I'm being tested and I need to seek God's guidance. If I push aside those feelings and try to find a solution my own way, I know I'll fail the test. If I stop, pray, and seek God's answer, he will guide me through what I'm facing with flying colors!

Anyone who has ever taken a big exam knows, if you study hard, you'll pass the test. Next time I'm facing God's testing, you better believe I'm pulling out my Bible and studying his Word because this is one test I definitely want to pass. If I do, I know there will be blessings and joy on earth as well as rewards in heaven coming my way.

---

[2] Genesis 22

"Trust in the Lord with all thine heart; and lean not unto thine own understanding. In all thy ways acknowledge him, and he shall direct thy paths" (Proverbs 3:5–6).

"Study to shew thyself approved unto God, a workman that needeth not to be ashamed, rightly dividing the word of truth" (2 Timothy 2:15).

"And the scripture was fulfilled which saith, Abraham believed God, and it was imputed unto him for righteousness: and he was called the Friend of God" (James 2:23).

"Knowing this, that the trying of your faith worketh patience. But let patience have her perfect work, that ye may be perfect and entire, wanting nothing" (James 1:3–4).

REDO

One day I was sitting in my room with the windows open when I heard some neighborhood kids playing outside. It sounded like they were playing baseball. Whenever one of the kids didn't hit the ball the way he wanted to, he'd yell "Redo!" Before you know it, after every hit, I heard "Redo!" I laughed to myself thinking, *If all they have is redos, how do they ever get to play the game?*

It made me realize something. How many times has God given me a redo in life? Our God is a God of forgiveness and second chances. He makes it easy for us to come to him with a heavy heart full of guilt and regret. He stands with his arms wide open, welcoming us with love and acceptance. There is nothing he won't forgive or wash away under the precious blood his Son, Jesus, shed on the cross for us. He gives us a new life in him when we ask Jesus to come into our hearts and accept him as our Savior.

God always gives us a chance to make things right in our lives. The parents who feel they weren't always there for their children get a chance to love and provide for them. The husbands who feel they weren't attentive to their wives get a chance to love and embrace them. The children who have strayed from their family get a chance to come back to the loving arms of their parents. Those who need a second chance to find the right path in life gratefully find it.

Redos may seem to defeat the purpose of a baseball game, but when it comes to the road of life, redos are a way of God saying, "Now let's try this again, but this time I'll lead, and we'll do it together."

I'm so glad God gives us a redo when we need it the most.

"And he that sat upon the throne said, Behold, I make all things new. And he said unto me, Write: for these words are true and faithful" (Revelation 21:5).

"Ask, and it shall be given you; seek, and ye shall find; knock, and it shall be opened unto you" (Matthew 7:7).

"But Jesus beheld them, and said unto them, With men this is impossible; but with God all things are possible" (Matthew 19:26).

"If we confess our sins, he is faithful and just to forgive us our sins, and to cleanse us from all unrighteousness" (1 John 1:9).

SECOND CHANCES

A second chance is a new start in life. That is what some hope for. Our God is a God of second chances and new beginnings. He proved that in the life of one woman, Patti, who thought all hope was lost in her life. Patti found herself in a rehab center for drug and alcohol addiction. After years of struggling, she surrendered to God, and he saved her and gave her a second chance at life. He led her down a path to trusting him as her Lord and Savior. Her faith and trust was restored in her higher power, Jesus.

While in rehab, she was made to run out in the fields to get exercise. She felt energized running out there on the open fields. Little did she know the very fields she ran on, her grandson would one day run on for soccer practice years later.

Even in her darkest times, God was working and laying out his plans for her future. Years had passed, and she became a great soul winner and spiritual influence on her family. The rehab center eventually closed, and the land was sold. A Christian school looking for a permanent home bought it. It was that very school where her grandson, Noah, attended and graduated from. I, her daughter, am currently working there. There, our family has experienced so many great blessings from God and have come full circle.

You see our God is a God of second chances. He even gives a piece of land and an old building a second chance to be used for his glory and honor. He turned an old rehab hospital into a place of hope and healing for a broken family.

Our God is a God of hope and grace. Whether we've had bad times in our lives, experienced true hardships, or just simply had a stressful day at work, we must always remember in the end that he is there for us to hang on to. He brings an everlasting hope and peace in our hearts. It is never too late for second chances with Jesus.

"I waited patiently for the LORD; and he inclined unto me, and heard my cry. He brought me up also out of an horrible pit, out of the miry clay, and set my feet upon a rock, and established my goings" (Psalm 40:1–2).

"It is of the Lord's mercies that we are not consumed, because his compassions fail not. They are new every morning: great is thy faithfulness" (Lamentations 3:22–23).

"And he said unto me, My grace is sufficient for thee: for my strength is made perfect in weakness. Most gladly therefore will I rather glory in my infirmities, that the power of Christ may rest upon me" (2 Corinthains 12:9).

"For ye were as sheep going astray; but are now returned unto the Shepherd and Bishop of your souls" (1 Peter 2:25).

I dedicate this devotional to my mom, Patti Smith. May her glory story live on and inspire others.

STEALING PRECIOUS MOMENTS

If you give a child a toy, he will be bored in thirty minutes or less. If you give him an empty box, he will be entertained for days. Who knew a box could provide so much fun? The power of the box can even bring a parent and child together for a moment to laugh with one another.

For some time now, I had been trying to find ways to spend time with my son and build a stronger relationship with him. He sat on the couch one Sunday afternoon with an empty box on his lap.

"Look! Can you see her nose?" He was referring to our cat's face poking through a hole in the box.

Our cat loves sitting in boxes. My son tried putting his finger in the hole, and we burst out laughing as we watched her paw stick out and try to grab his finger. So there we were, laughing and sharing a moment on a quiet Sunday afternoon, and all it took was an empty box and a playful cat to bring us together. In a world where life is so busy that it goes by like a speeding train, we have to stop from time to time and steal a few minutes here and there to make time for one another.

That's what it was like for Jesus. When the city around him was quiet early in the morning or in the evening, he departed alone and went to a solitary place to pray. He would take the time before a busy day to get alone with his heavenly Father. He would also take time during the evening hours and pour out his heart to God and be filled with the Holy Spirit.

We too need to take time each day to get alone with our heavenly Father to empty ourselves before him so he could fill us with his hope, love, and grace. There is no greater time well spent than to steal precious moments with our Lord.

"And in the morning, rising up a great while before day, he went out, and departed into a solitary place, and there prayed" (Mark 1:35).

"And when he had sent the multitudes away, he went up into a mountain apart to pray: and when the evening was come, he was there alone" (Matthew 14:23).

"Draw nigh to God, and he will draw nigh to you" (James 4:8).

"Seek ye the LORD while he may be found, call ye upon him while he is near" (Isaiah 55:6).

STILL, SMALL VOICE

There was that nagging feeling again. It was 1:30 a.m. when a sense of overwhelming anxiety awakened me. Something was wrong. What was causing this feeling? It was agonizing. It was like a lump in my throat that wouldn't go away.

I kept asking God, "What is it? What's wrong?" I have felt this feeling before. Either I did something wrong or didn't do something I was supposed to. I was starting to get angry and upset. I didn't know what God was trying to tell me.

There was a fear that this horrible feeling was caused by me taking the new job I was offered. Could this be a big mistake? Did God not want me to take this job? Everyone around me was praying I would get it. We all believed it was God's will. So now why was I feeling a strong pull from the Holy Spirit that something was terribly wrong?

My answer came in the mail yesterday when a letter arrived stating that my son's medical insurance was being shut off in a matter of days. It was then that the realization came to me that God was telling me I forgot to do something important, and now we were in trouble.

With all the busyness of wrapping up my summer job, I was neglecting my job at home. I forgot all about the paperwork that was supposed to be sent in for my son's insurance. The August 3 deadline had come and gone! How could I be that careless and forgetful? What happened?

The answer to that question came so clearly to me. I neglected my personal time with God. Only through the quiet time of Bible reading and prayer is one refreshed mentally and physically. Taking that time each day has helped me to draw closer to my loving Savior, Jesus. It's only then that he is able to lead my life and help me to be a better person. If I get too busy and put off that time with him, then the distractions of this world keep me from hearing that still, small voice that he uses to guide me.

His still, small voice comes in different ways. It may be a thought he brings to mind. Or he may speak to me in a Bible verse that I really needed to read at the moment. If I don't take the time to be alone with him, then I will miss out on what he has to say.

God gives us the guidance and help we need to get through our daily lives. When we try to live without him, we may be missing out on some very important instructions, like the message of his gift of salvation through Jesus.

Take time each and every day to draw closer to God to dive into his precious Word, to feel his love around you, to reach out to him in prayer, and to experience hearing his still, small voice.

"And thine ears shall hear a word behind thee, saying, This is the way, walk ye in it, when ye turn to the right hand, and when ye turn to the left" (Isa. 30:21).

"He restoreth my soul: he leadeth me in the paths of righteousness for his name's sake" (Ps. 23:4).

"He that dwelleth in the secret place of the most High shall abide under the shadow of the Almighty" (Ps. 91:1).

"And after the earthquake a fire; but the LORD was not in the fire: and after the fire a still small voice" (1 Kings 19:12).

SUNSETS AND FIREWORKS

There is nothing like watching a good display of fireworks on a warm summer night. This past summer, I had the opportunity to watch the Fourth of July fireworks with my son and stepfather. It was a great experience being there with my family and sitting under the night sky. The sky lit up right over our heads with a burst of many colors. It was so loud that you could feel it boom in your chest.

It was an exciting experience, but I couldn't help but feel that, no matter how bright and beautiful this man-made display was, it was nothing compared to the beauty God made in this world. Fireworks are great to watch, but my favorite thing to watch in the sky are sunsets. For years, I have wondered if I were the only one to stop in the parking lot after coming out of the local grocery store just to gaze up at the beautiful display of orange and pink clouds. Sunsets are so calming and last far longer than one has time to sit and enjoy them.

God has taught me that we will have sunsets and fireworks in life. Fireworks represent those exciting times that only last a moment. Maybe it's a first date or kiss, a night out with friends, or even a chance to do something wild. Fireworks may feel amazing at the time, but they are short-lived, and the satisfaction never really lasts.

Sunsets represent the times and seasons that God brings in our lives when we wait on him and live in his will, for example, waiting on him to show you the right person to marry, career choice, or place to live.

To me, they represent experiencing the blessings he brings to us when we need them most. To some people, sunsets might not seem as exciting as fireworks, but if you trust God with your life, he will bring you comfort and joy greater than any feeling you can ever experience. God's sunsets last a lifetime.

Lately it seems like when I am having a real bad day and am overwhelmed with what is going on in my life, I see the brightest and most beautiful sunsets fill the sky. It's like God is saying, "No matter what happened that day, I still have everything in my hands."

There are those who live their lives always looking for fireworks. As for me, I will watch for sunsets.

"Thou wilt keep him in perfect peace, whose mind is stayed on thee: because he trusteth in thee. Trust ye in the LORD forever: for in the LORD JEHOVAH is everlasting strength" (Isaiah 26:3–4).

"Thus saith the LORD, Stand ye in the ways, and see, and ask for the old paths, where is the good way, and walk therein, and ye shall find rest for your souls" (Jerermiah 6:16).

"Call unto me, and I will answer thee, and shew thee great and mighty things, which thou knowest not" (Jeremiah 33:3).

"The LORD is good unto them that wait for him, to the soul that seeketh him" (Lamentations 3:25).

THE JOYS OF A RAINY DAY

When the rain comes, many blessings come with it. Rain is free water from God above to water our flowers and lawns. It also gives us a day of rest from all the hard outdoor work there is to do. It brings an opportunity to sit back and watch the garden get the water it greatly needs. Rain brings water to wash our green, pollen-covered cars with no cost and no effort.

For some people, rainy days give them a good reason to work inside the home for a while so they can clean out those closets and wash those floors. They get a chance to be inside with the cool breeze coming through.

Rainy days also give us a chance to curl up on the couch with a good book and a furry friend. The sound of the rain hitting the ground brings a calming peace that everyone stops to hear. Families get together to play games and bake cookies.

God brings us rainy days for many reasons. Most importantly, he knows we need the water, a life source for us here on earth, one we can't live without. God knows we are in need of another type of water as well. That is why Jesus came to earth, so he could give us *living water*, the precious gift of his salvation, a gift he purchased for us when he shed his blood and died on the cross for our sins.

Jesus's *living water* gives us a cleansing bath and washes away all our sins and wrongdoings. It brings us hope in uncertain times and frees us from all the guilt we once bore. It provides us with a new way to live and gives us a purpose to keep on living. His *living water* is as abundant as the rain that falls from the sky. All we have to do is open our hearts and receive it.

"Jesus answered and said unto her, If thou knewest the gift of God and who it is that saith to thee, Give me to drink; thou wouldest have asked of him, and he would have given thee living water" (John 4:10).

"Jesus answered and said unto her, Whosoever drinketh of this water shall thirst again: But whosoever drinketh of the water that I shall give him shall never thirst; but the water that I shall give him shall be in him a well of water springing up into everlasting life" (John 4:13–14).

"The thief cometh not, but for to steal, and to kill, and to destroy: I am come that they might have life, and that they might have it more abundantly" (John 10:10).

"He that hath the Son hath life; and he that hath not the Son of God hath not life" (1 John 5:12).

THE TRUE MEANING
OF CHRISTMAS

There is so much to see and do at Christmastime that you really use all of your five senses to their full potential. Out of all five senses, which is your favorite to use during the holiday season? Is it the sense of smell, where you catch a whiff of all the cookies, cakes, and desserts cooking? Is it smelling the scented candles burning and that fresh pine aroma of wreaths and Christmas trees? Or how about your sense of taste when you get to eat all those baked cookies, desserts, and holiday meals? How about the sense of hearing when you hear Christmas carols playing on the radio, in the stores, at church, and at concerts?

My favorite is using my sense of sight. I love looking at Christmas decorations and lights on the houses at night in my neighborhood. I used to take my son for a drive at night so we could try to find the house with the most lights on it. Oh, and there's Christmas trees. I just love looking at Christmas trees. I could sit for hours gazing at them. They are so beautiful.

Last year, I was so caught up in decorating my house, putting up the Christmas tree, and running around buying gifts that I forgot about the true meaning of Christmas. What is the true meaning of Christmas? Well, it's to celebrate the birth of our Savior, Jesus.

See, God had a perfect plan. He knows we are all sinners. The Bible says, "For all have sinned and come short of the glory of God." God is a just and righteous God, which means he is full of truth and he is upright and faithful. He is perfect and holy. He can't allow sin to come into heaven.

When Jesus came to earth to take the punishment for our sin, that meant that God could still be a just and righteous judge and still welcome us into heaven because he sees us as clean and perfect through Jesus's blood. Jesus took the punishment for all our sins when he died on the cross so we could be innocent and guiltless. We can then be found just and righteous in God's eyes.

That's why Christmas is such an important holiday. It is the day we celebrate Jesus coming down to this earth to be born as a human in order to sacrifice himself on the cross as our loving Savior.

So this Christmas, as you use your five senses and enjoy all the festivities that Christmas brings, be sure to stop and remember the true meaning of Christmas, the birth of Jesus, our Savior and Lord.

"For all have sinned, and come short of the glory of God; Being justified freely by his grace through the redemption that is in Christ Jesus" (Romans 3:23–24).

"For God so loved the world, that he gave his only begotten Son, that whosoever believeth in him should not perish, but have everlasting life" (John 3:16).

"For unto you is born this day in the city of David a Saviour, which is Christ the Lord" (Luke 2:11).

"The Lord is not slack concerning his promise, as some men count slackness; but is longsuffering to us-ward, not willing that any should perish, but that all should come to repentance" (2 Peter 3:9).

TIMING IS EVERYTHING

It was Friday afternoon. I couldn't wait to get home. I was so happy. Our town was going out trick-or-treating that night. Even though my son and I haven't done anything for Halloween in years, this year I decided to take advantage of the opportunity of having people come to my door. So I made little invitations to hand out to the kids, inviting them to come to Sunday school.

Unfortunately I was working in the aftercare program at school that evening and had to stay late. I was frustrated because we only had one student and two adults. Needless to say, my coworker and I really wanted to go home early. At the same time, my son was waiting at the school to get his senior pictures taken.

Finally after 5:30 p.m., we could all go home. My son and I left the parking lot at the same time. On the way home, I prayed about handing out my church invites and hoped I didn't miss too many trick-or-treaters. Suddenly as I was waiting for a red light to turn green, I felt my car jolt forward. The car behind me slammed into the back of my car. As soon as the light turned green, I pulled into a parking lot and took a look at the damage.

I couldn't help but think the devil did not want me to hand out those invitations to church. Strangely enough, I wasn't upset or stressed. Peace came over me. It didn't seem like a big deal to me. I knew everything would be fine. I calmly exchanged my information with the other driver and went on my way. I knew this untimely event was all in God's hands.

When I got home, my son asked me what happened. He told me he was behind the car that hit me. It wasn't until later that night that I burst into tears when I realized something important. If I hadn't pulled out of the parking lot first, my car might have been behind the accident, and my son might have been the one that was in the accident. I would have been devastated if I saw the car in front of me hit my son. As I thought about it more, I realized, if I hadn't worked late that evening at all, my son might have been in that accident without me even knowing.

God's timing is always perfect, even when bad things happen. I was grateful it was my car that was hit and that I saw my son's car pass by me and head safely home. I even got home in time to hand out all my Sunday school invitations. I know God's hand is still on this troubling situation and he will have everything work out with my car getting repaired. I thank him for his perfect timing. He will always be there for us from beginning to end.

"And he said unto them, It is not for you to know the times or the seasons, which the Father hath put in his own power" (Acts 1:7).

"The LORD *also will be a refuge for the oppressed, a refuge in times of trouble. And they that know thy name will put their trust in thee: for thou,* LORD, *hast not forsaken them that seek thee"* (Psalm 9:9–10).

"To every thing there is a season, and a time to every purpose under the heaven" (Ecclesiastes 3:1).

"He hath made every thing beautiful in his time: also he hath set the world in their heart, so that no man can find out the work that God maketh from the beginning to the end" (Ecclesiastes 3:11).

WHAT DOES GOD
MEAN TO YOU?

If someone were to ask you who God is, what would you say? What does he mean to you?

It's hard to find a person in the world who hasn't heard of God. I find it absolutely fascinating that, if you were to travel to the deepest parts of the Amazon jungle and find an indigenous tribe, you would see they have a desire to worship something greater than themselves. They have a desire to believe in some type of god. Hmm, it makes you think. Don't we all have that desire whether we want to admit it or not?

If I were to walk up to people on the street and ask them if they know who God is, I would get all kinds of answers. Some people would say, "He's the man upstairs" or "He's some great big mysterious being that no one really knows." Agnostics would tell me they heard of him but aren't sure he really exists or not. Atheists would tell me that he doesn't exist. They simply refuse to believe in him.

Some religions believe in God and have a lot to say about him. They even pray to him and say his name over and over, but as they walk out the door after church service, God is put back on the shelf until the following week. He is left out of their daily lives until they need something from him.

I have noticed that some people only believe in God when they need someone to blame or get angry at. Other people just downright hate God, and some don't even know the reason why.

My mom was one of those people. At one point and time in her life, she would tell people, as long as God stayed out of her way and she stayed out of his, they'd be fine. That was until one day when a friend of hers told her how much God loved her. God drew her to him right at that moment, and they had a close personal relationship ever since. I'll tell more of my mom's story later. For now, let me tell you what God means to me.

God is my rock and my shield, my creator and my loving Savior, my protector and my guide. He is the one who loves me more than I'll ever know. He is the only one who forgives me before I even ask him to. His has the power to wash away all my sins. He is the provider for all my needs. He is the peace that passeth all understanding. He is the greatest comforter I could ever have. He is my reason for living and my great inspiration for life. He is my joy and my crown. His name is Jesus, and I hope you seek him and get to know him like I do. He will change your life for the better.

"But thou, O Lord, art a shield for me; my glory, and the lifter up of mine head" (Psalm 3:3).

"Jesus saith unto him, I am the way, the truth, and the life: no man cometh unto the Father, but by me" (John 14:6).

"For as much as there is none like unto thee, O LORD; thou art great, and thy name is great in might" (Jeremiah 10:6).

"To whom then will ye liken me, or shall I be equal? saith the Holy One. Lift up your eyes on high, and behold who hath created these things, that bringeth out their host by number: he calleth them all by names by the greatness of his might, for that he is strong in power; not one faileth" (Isaiah 40:25–26).

O-Others

In a society where it's all about me, it's hard to put ourselves aside for the needs of others. Oh, but when we do, we help make this world a better place—a kind smile to a stranger or a helping hand to someone in need. Every time we stretch out our hand to be there for someone else, we show the love of God through us.

Jesus himself left his heavenly home to come to earth to teach, minister, suffer, die, and victoriously rise again. He did this for us, not himself. He is the ultimate picture of what happens when you put others first.

In this next section, I want to share with you what God has taught me when it comes to thinking of others first.

A DIAMOND IN THE ROUGH

As the school year starts off, there is nothing but joy in my heart as I see the students smiling in the hallway. Do they know how blessed they are to be in a Christian school filled with teachers who have a strong love and faith in the Lord?

Picture a classroom starting to get a little too noisy and active. The teacher pauses and asks the students to take a moment to settle down and pray. Silence settles over the room as each head is bowed and they are lifted up to God for help and guidance. Moments like these truly warm my heart.

Each day I notice something new and special about my new school, but today something really hit home. I wish that every child could have an opportunity to go to a Christian school. There is a common problem among Christian schools in New England though. They lack the funds needed to support students with special academic needs. It is unfortunate as students with disabilities, whether physical or learning, need the spiritual support of a Christian school just as much, if not more, than students without disabilities.

They need to know how much Jesus loves them and how, as their loving Savior, he can help them overcome the struggles they face in life. I can't help but wonder how many children would like to be in a Christian school but feel they aren't able to.

We all have at one point in time faced some type of rejection or have felt like an outcast in different areas of our lives. For kids, it's trying out for a sports team or play. For adults, it's when we apply for a job and are turned down. We feel like we aren't good enough, fast enough, talented enough, smart enough, or even educated enough.

No matter what the world thinks, Jesus will always see us as good enough for the role he has for us in life. Aren't you glad he gives us a chance to be more than what we appear to be and that we can accomplish great things through him?

He knows each one of us inside and out. He created us and loves us more than we'll ever know. We may be sinners that need to be washed in his blood and polished up a bit, but in God's eyes, we are all more precious than gold.

Even diamonds as beautiful and sparkling as they appear to be were once soiled, black pieces of coal. Over time with the help of God's hand on our lives, we too can be found as a diamond in the rough.

Just think of Helen Keller. How many people would have turned her away if Ann Sullivan hadn't taken the time to work with her? If God can perform such amazing miracles in that young girl's life and make her to become the heroic, inspirational woman she turned out to be, then God can work in any person's life and have him or her achieve great things. We just need to invite God into our hearts and let his work begin.

"Don't ever let anyone get you down and make you feel like you're not good enough. Just remember, "I can do all things through Christ, which strengtheneth me" (Phil. 4:13).

"Why art thou cast down, O my soul? and why art thou disquieted within me? hope thou in God: for I shall yet praise him, who is the health of my countenance, and my God" (Psalm 42:11).

"What shall we then say to these things? If God be for us, who can be against us?" (Romans 8:31).

"Let your conversation be without covetousness; and be content with such things as ye have: for he hath said, I will never leave thee, nor forsake thee. So that we may boldly say, The Lord is my helper, and I will not fear what man shall do unto me" (Hebrews 13:5–6).

A MESSAGE WITH URGENCY

My son and I were camping this week with friends when I suddenly awoke with a sense of urgency on the last morning. It started to rain on the morning we were to leave. I jumped up around 5:00 a.m. and started getting things packed up. God had blessed us by holding off the rain until the last day. I was grateful for that, but I knew he was telling me to get going before it started to pour. Thankfully we got everything in the car in time and only got a little wet before the heavy rains came.

While I was packing up our stuff, I felt God was reminding me of another sense of urgency. I felt such a rush to pack up and protect our stuff from the rain, but as I was packing, I realized I should be this eager when it comes to reaching out to those in trouble before it's too late. I started thinking about this when we all went out to lunch the day before. My son mentioned that Robin Williams, the well-known famous actor, had committed suicide. From what I hear, he had a battle with depression.

There had been times in my life when I battled depression on and off. It affected every area of my life, including my relationships and my ability to be a mother to my son. The urgency I feel now is due to God telling me to reach out to those who are going through what I have endured. At one point, I lost all hope. I found myself on the kitchen floor with a bottle of alcohol and a bottle of Tylenol PM, begging God to knock me out long enough to take away the pain.

That is when I finally surrendered my life to Jesus and asked him to forgive me of my sins and come into my heart as my Savior and Lord of my life. I told him I wanted to do things his way, not mine, anymore. In his mercy and love, he picked me up and dusted me off, and he has taken care of me ever since. Now I know he allowed me to go through all that so I could bring hope to others who are feeling there is no hope.

As we see in the life of Robin Williams as well as other famous people, the world will promise you riches, fame, and happiness but will leave you empty inside. I learned the hard way that there is nothing in this world that will fill me up and bring me true happiness outside of Jesus, my Savior. I have a sense of urgency to let people know he is their true joy and their blessed hope and he died to cleanse them of all their sins once and for all.

No matter what you are battling in life, just know that you are so precious to him and he wants to help you and show you how much he loves you. He saved my life, and it's up to me with urgency to tell you he can save your life too. Don't lose hope. Find Jesus instead.

"And they said, Believe on the Lord Jesus Christ, and thou shalt be saved, and thy house" (Acts 16:31).

"Be of good courage, and he shall strengthen your heart, all ye that hope in the LORD" (Psalm 31:24).

"Behold, the Lord GOD will come with strong hand, and his arm shall rule for him: behold, his reward is with him, and his work before him" (Isaiah 40:10).

"And let us not be weary in well doing: for in due season we shall reap, if we faint not" (Galatians 6:9).

A MOTHER'S FAITH

A mother's faith and God's mighty hand are a combination that can shake the world.

"How?" you might ask.

When a mother prays, she comes to her knees and brings the burdens of her heart to the one who has created the heavens and the earth, the one who can take every sorrowful request and do mighty things when he answers.

Many famous preachers and evangelists had a strong, faithful mother somewhere behind the scenes praying for them. Before God mightily used some of those men, the situation looked grim. It seemed like all was lost in their children's lives. These mothers clung to their faith, believed the promises of God's Word, and cried out to their Lord and Savior on behalf of their sons and daughters. Through their faith and unending love, God moved to stir the hardest of hearts. They never gave up, stopped praying, and ceased believing in the power of God.

Hudson Taylor, the founder of the China Inland Mission, was convinced that he could never be saved so he decided to live a worldly life.[3] His mother locked herself in a room one day and was determined she would not leave until her prayers were answered that her son would be converted. Unbeknownst to her, miles away, her son, Hudson, was reading a tract and came to salvation through Jesus while she was praying.

We all know that well-known hymn, "Amazing Grace," by John Newton. Little do some people know, John Newton was once a wicked man. He ran away from home as a rebellious teen.[4] His father disowned him for his wicked behavior, and he became a drunken sailor that got involved with slave trading.

While all of this was going on, John Newton's mother prayed through many tears for the salvation of her son. She kept praying for him, and one day, John

---

[3] Eugene Myers Harrison, "J. Hudson Taylor: God's Mighty Man of Prayer," accessed April 29, 2017, http://www.wholesomewords.org/missions/biotaylor3.html.
[4] "A Godly Mother Ain't Like No Other," accessed April 29, 2017, http://www.preacherscorner.org/wagers-mother.htm.

came to know Jesus as his Savior, and his life was changed. God used John Newton to reach thousands of people for Christ. He truly "was once lost and then found" with the help of his mother's prayers.

Pauline Hamilton was a great missionary. When she was young, her parents dedicated her to God to be used as a missionary to China. They named her after the great apostle Paul.[5] At one point in Pauline's life, it didn't look like their hopes and dreams for her would come true. A rebellious Pauline got into drugs and alcohol. She became depressed and decided to commit suicide one day. She ran out of the house, ignored her mother calling after her, jumped in her car, and headed down the road with the intention of driving off a steep cliff.

On the way, her tire blew out, and she took it as a sign that God saved her life.[6] She came to know Christ and gave the rest of her life to serve him. Pauline was a member of the China Inland Mission. She ministered to thousands of men, women, and youth. She had a great impact on ministering to delinquent street boys. Her mother never gave up praying for her.

God wants every mother to know he hears our prayers. Our prodigal children can never go beyond the reach of our prayers and the powerful hand of God. With a mother's faith and trust in the Lord, they will come back. Keep praying, don't give up, and strengthen your faith by surrendering to the Lord. And you will see God work in the lives of your children.

Oh, how far my son may go, but he will never be out of your reach, Lord.

---

[5] "Pauline G. Hamilton 1915 ~ 1988," accessed May 1, 2017, http://womenofchristianity. com/pauline-g-hamilton-1915-1988.
[6] P. Hamilton, *To a Different Drum* (Toronto: Overseas Missionary Fellowship, 1984).

"And all things, whatsoever ye shall ask in prayer, believing, ye shall receive" (Matthew 21:22).

"And whatsoever ye shall ask in my name, that will I do, that the Father may be glorified in the Son. If ye shall ask any thing in my name, I will do it" (John 14:13–14).

"Be careful for nothing; but in every thing by prayer and supplication with thanksgiving let your requests be made known unto God" (Philippians 4:6).

"When I call to remembrance the unfeigned faith that is in thee, which dwelt first in thy grandmother Lois, and thy mother Eunice; and I am persuaded that is in thee also" (2 Timothy 1:4).

A VETERAN'S HEART

On a day like Veteran's Day, we choose to honor those who have made a commitment to serve and give their lives for their country. Our military are made up of a group of brave men and women who are also selfless, honorable, and loyal.

My mother once said the only regret she had in life was that she did not serve in the armed forces. She had a heart for the military and American veterans. When she watched the news and caught a glimpse of the names of the people who died in serving their country, she would say, "Well done, thou good and faithful soldier."

Even though she did not serve in the United States military, she did serve in the Lord's army. When she was the weakest and most susceptible to her illness, she was the greatest witness for her Lord and Savior, Jesus. In the back of her Bible was a list of over five hundred names of people, all of which she gave the gospel to.

God can use the most surprising people. Corrie Ten Boom, a great speaker and missionary for the Lord herself, met a woman who couldn't move or speak. The only thing she could do was move one finger.

You might think, *How awful, that poor woman. What quality of life does she have?* To be honest, God used her to do the most amazing work. You see, this woman was so sick that she was unable to move, but she could type with that one finger, and she did. She gave God her all, and she spent many hours typing and translating the Bible into her own language.

Because of her faith and work, many people were able to secretly get a hold of a copy of the Bible during a time after World War II when Christians in her country were persecuted and killed. Since she was in such poor health, she was never a suspect in her work. She was a true wounded soldier for Christ.

Many prayer warriors are behind great revivals and strong preachers. It takes one small person to pray and call upon God's great power to move on this earth.

Are you broken, lost, sick, or wounded? You are still a precious child in God's eyes. You too can be a wounded soldier for a great cause, a wounded soldier for the Lord. One day you will hear, "Well done, thou good and faithful servant."

"His lord said unto him, Well done, good and faithful servant; thou hast been faithful over a few things, I will make thee ruler over many things: enter thou into the joy of thy lord" (Matthew 25:23)

"Thou therefore endure hardness, as a good soldier of Jesus Christ" (2 Timothy 2:3)

"For this day is holy unto our Lord: neither be ye sorry; for the joy of the LORD is your strength" (Nehemiah 8:10).

"And let us not be weary in well doing: for in due season we shall reap, if we faint not" (Galations 6:9).

ARE YOU ON A CRUSADE?

They came on horses with armor and swords in their hands. Their eyes focused on God, or so they thought. To them, their intentions were honorable, but to the Lord, they were off the mark. The Crusades were a time when men of God came to the Middle East to claim the Holy Land. They brought the sword of war instead of the sword of God's Word. They came to fight the heathen instead of giving them the love and compassion that Jesus once gave them.

Imagine if the crusaders were missionaries instead of men of war. How different would the Middle East be right now? What if, instead of marching in and trying to take over the land, they surrendered to the Lord and served God in that area? Say they built churches and homes for the people and took care of their sick. What an impact that would have made. Perhaps more people would have come to know Jesus as their Savior and there would be more peace and less fighting in the Middle East.

The crusaders thought they were doing right by God. But their intentions were wrong. They were more about pride than God's will. Some Christians today tend to have the same tendencies. We go out in the world ready to convert people and change lives for Christ. Unfortunately we sometimes lack the compassion that comes from the one who lead us by example.

Jesus did not come to conquer. He came to serve and surrender for the sake of others. Followers of Christ are to do the same. They are to serve the people around them and surrender to God's will for their lives. All we do in life is to be done with the same unconditional love Jesus had.

The name Christian means "follower of Christ." Let's live out that name and Jesus Christ's example by serving others.

"If ye keep my commandments, ye shall abide in my love; even as I have kept my Father's commandments, and abide in his love" (John 15:10).

"No man hath seen God at any time. If we love one another, God dwelleth in us, and his love is perfected in us" (1 John 4:12).

"Herein is our love made perfect, that we may have boldness in the day of judgment: because as he is, so are we in this world" (1 John 4:17).

"Finally, brethren, farewell. Be perfect, be of good comfort, be of one mind, live in peace; and the God of love and peace shall be with you" (2 Corinthians 13:11).

DON'T GIVE UP ON ME

Have you ever heard a struggling family member say, "Don't give up on me"? Have you ever had an argument with a rebellious teen? Finding it hard to stand firm, you gaze into his or her eyes and see a pleading look almost say, "Don't give up on me."

Have you ever had it out with your spouse, where you are both so frustrated that you become exhausted? You let your own feelings go just long enough to hear his or her heart say, "Don't give up on me."

Now I ask you, "Have you spent long hours in sorrow dwelling on the troubles in your life?" You pause for a moment and hear God softly whisper, "I can take care of you. Don't give up on me."

When we feel like giving up on others, ourselves, and even God, we need to remember God's love for us. There is nothing we can't face or overcome when we have the unconditional love of God in our hearts. We can trust him.

When Jesus faced the agony of the cross, he did it out of love. He saw the world and all the sin that was in it, but he never gave up on us. He showed us how much he loved us by suffering and dying on the cross so we can be free from the burden of our sin. We can live with the hope of eternity in paradise with him. He loves us no matter what we do. Nothing can separate us from him.

When we ask Jesus to come into our hearts to be our Lord and Savior, he lives through us and brings his unconditional love with him. His love encourages us to not give up on others when they fall. That same love also reminds us not to give up on him when times get rough. God promises to never leave us nor forsake us. No matter what. When I face the challenge of loving someone when he or she upsets me, God reminds me to love others as he loves me.

So remember God's love for you and tell that struggling family member, "I'm here for you. I won't give up on you." Take that rebellious teen in a loving embrace and say, "I love you. I won't give up on you." Hold your spouse and promise not to let go. Comfort your spouse and show the one you love that you won't give up.

Most importantly, let God take all your cares and woes into his hands. Trust Jesus as Lord and Savior of your life, and say, "I need you. I won't give up hope."

Jesus reassures us of his great love for us in the Bible and encourages us to keep up the faith and trust him. Always remember that he will never give up on you.

"Nor height, nor depth, nor any other creature, shall be able to separate us from the love of God, which is in Christ Jesus our Lord" (Romans 8:39).

"There is no fear in love; but perfect love casteth out fear" (1 John 4:18).

"Let your conversation be without covetousness; and be content with such things as ye have: for he hath said, I will never leave thee, nor forsake thee" (Hebrews 13:5).

"We love him, because he first loved us" (1 John 4:19).

LET HIM SAIL

Last summer, my son and I were given the opportunity to take sailing lessons for free. It was such an exciting experience. There is nothing quite like sailing on a warm summer evening. What a joy to breathe in the salty air while the shimmery water surrounds us. We even watched the sunset as we sailed around New Castle, New Hampshire. I was so grateful and thanked God for this chance with my son. I was really enjoying each lesson until my fun turned to fear one day.

The last day of our lessons was extremely windy. I overheard one of our instructors mention a risk of gale-force winds. We could barely get our small sailboats ready and into the water. One of the ropes on the sail kept whipping me. Once we were in the water, our boat kept tipping from one side to the other. Our instructor was calm and told us that was normal, but I was hanging on for dear life. I kept praying to God, "Please don't let us capsize."

I looked over at my son and worried about how afraid he might be. I found myself giving him orders instead of letting him listen to the instructor. I let my fear take over. When the lesson was over and we were on dry land again, I finally stopped shaking. I kept thanking God that we were safe and back on solid ground.

Despite our one scary adventure, my son and I really enjoyed sailing together. I learned a lot more during that whole experience than just how to sail a 420 sailboat. God taught me there will come a time in my son's life when I need to let go and let him sail on his own.

As a mom, I can teach him what he needs to know to live a godly life and help him map out his course. I can give him the tools he needs to use to be successful, such as reading the Bible, praying, and going to church. I can show him how to trust Jesus as his Savior and to encourage him to make Jesus the captain of his life. I can trust the wind of the Holy Spirit to blow my son in the right direction. Then I can stand on the shore and pray for him as I watch him take off.

I now realize I may not like every direction he's going in. I know it will be hard to stand and watch him go through the storms. I learned that it's during those times that I need to take a step back and let my son listen to God as he directs his paths. It won't do him any good if I am shouting orders at him as he travels through rough seas. The best thing I can do is prepare a secure foundation for him while he's with me. Then when the time comes, I must have faith and trust God to take over as I let him sail.

"Train up a child in the way he will go: and when he is old, he will not depart from it" (Proverbs 22:6).

"But Jesus beheld them, and said unto them, With men this is impossible; but with God all things are possible" (Matthew 19:26).

"And, ye fathers, provoke not your children to wrath: but bring them up in the nurture and admonition of the Lord" (Ephesians 6:4).

"I will instruct thee and teach thee in the way which thou shalt go: I will guide thee with mine eye" (Psalm 32:8).

ME AND MY SHADOW

One day I walked into my son's room and was disappointed to see his dirty clothes laying all over the floor. I didn't say anything to him. I just shook my head and walked away. As I walked into my room, I suddenly stopped. I was shocked to see my own dirty clothes laying in piles here and there on the floor. That's when I realized I was frustrated with him for something I do myself.

I asked myself, "Are there other irritating things that my son does that I also do without realizing it?" Yes, there is! I was surprised to hear how rudely I answered him one time when he asked me a question. Then I noticed how I also get angry over little things that don't really matter. I always got so frustrated with him when he did that. Finally I noticed that I have a bad habit of not looking at him when he's talking to me, and I will also start talking to him—or actually yelling to him—from another room instead of giving him my full attention.

All this time, I thought my son needed to work on the way he acts, but to be honest, he was just copying my behavior! I quickly realized, if I want him to behave a certain way, I need to change my own behavior and be a role model for him. He is my shadow.

As a parent, I create the patterns for his way of life. Some of those come from him following in my footsteps. The more I change the way I act, talk, and do things for the better, the more he notices and corrects his own behavior. Now I always ask God to help me stop, pray, and think before I speak and act. You never know when little shadows might be following you.

"She openeth her mouth with wisdom; and in her tongue is the law of kindness. She looketh well to the ways of her household, and eateth not the bread of idleness. Her children arise up and call her blessed" (Proverbs 31:26–28).

"The just man walketh in his integrity: his children are blessed after him" (Proverbs 20:7).

"Hear thou, my son, and be wise, and guide thine heart in the way" (Proverbs 23:19).

"My son, keep thy father's commandment, and forsake not the law of thy mother: Bind them continually upon thine heart, and tie them about thy neck" (Proverbs 6:20–21).

SEASON OF LOVE

The time between Christmas and Valentine's Day can seem like the longest, dreariest time of the year. It's cold, gray, and lifeless.

We mustn't focus on the cold or the barren grounds around us. No, we must hold on to the spark of love that Christmas brings into our hearts and feel the flame of that love grow deep within us as Valentine's Day approaches.

This is no ordinary love. This is true, powerful agape love, the amazing unconditional love that God has for us. His love fills our hearts as a blazing fire and pours out upon those around us.

Unconditional love is not something we have on our own. It helps to have God's love in our hearts first. It's easy to be happy on a sunny spring day. The warm sunshine and flowers blooming bring such joy. When the cold weather sets in, that happiness can become despair when the emptiness of winter is all you see. The same is with love. It's easy to love someone when he or she makes you happy. It's harder to love a person when he or she disappoints or hurts you.

That is when love is the most powerful though. True unconditional love means to love someone when it seems impossible to do so. Our love for family, friends, and others should be a love of action, not feeling. If we choose to love that person we are struggling to love and then act out that love with kindness and compassion, the result will bring a warm glow of joy in our hearts.

That is how God loves us. He loves us unconditionally. No matter what we do, he will always love us. He proved that to us by sending his Son Jesus to die on the cross to take away our sins. He loves us so much that he sacrificed his own Son to pay the penalty for our sins so we can go to heaven. What greater love could we possibly experience than that?

The little flakes of snow seem so tiny and delicate, but wow! Look at the job they can do together. The little acts of love we do for others may seem so small and insignificant but what an impact they will have on one's life. Love unconditionally this winter season and feel God's overwhelming love for you.

"This is my commandment, That ye love one another, as I have loved you" (John 15:12).

"He healeth the broken in heart, and bindeth up their wounds" (Psalm 147:3).

"Herein is love, not that we loved God, but that he loved us, and sent his Son to be the propitiation for our sins. Beloved, if God so loved us, we ought also to love one another" (1 John 4:10–11).

"But I say unto you, Love your enemies, bless them that curse you, do good to them that hate you, and pray for them which despitefully use you, and persecute you" (Matthew 5:44).

STAINS ON THE HEART

Standing on the edge of the shoreline, I could see and hear the waves crashing and smell the fresh salt air. It was a beautiful summer day, and my son and I were at our favorite beach in Rye, New Hampshire. My son was off jumping in the waves, one of his favorite things to do at the beach. He kept going further and further out into the deep water. I had told him to not go out too far. My frustration grew as I watched him. I started calling out to him, but with the wind and the sound of the waves, he couldn't hear me. I will never forget the look on his face as he turned around to look for me.

It wasn't until I saw a woman grabbing him and helping him to shore that I realized my son was struggling. The large waves and the force of the water was too strong for him. He couldn't get to shore on his own. God was looking out for my son that day and sent that woman to help him before he hit the rocks. Unfortunately I was more focused on my anger and frustration over my son not listening to me rather than on my son and his need to be rescued.

Sadly this was not the only time I put my emotions before my son. A couple of times, I got angry at him for spilling something on the carpet. At the time, getting the stains out of the carpet mattered more to me than my son's feelings. I wish it were the other way around.

Our first reaction to a frustrating situation involving our children may be one of anger. Stop, pray, and think before you speak and act. Our children will make mistakes, break things, and let us down from time to time. Why? Because they are sinners just like we are. Sometimes mistakes are a necessary part of growing and learning. In God's eyes, we as parents make mistakes and fail him as well. Oh, but how loving our God is to send his Son Jesus to die on the cross so he can forgive us for our sins so we can go to heaven one day.

God, as our loving heavenly Father, gives us a chance to repent and learn from our faults. As parents, we are to do the same and take each unhappy and frustrating moment with our children and turn it around by using it to teach and encourage them to make the right decisions in life.

The world is full of material things, like stained carpets that can be washed and broken knickknacks that can be replaced. But the stains of wrongful hurt and pain on a child's heart might never be taken away. Love your children at all costs, teach them with every experience you can, and always put them before yourself.

"And, ye fathers, provoke not your children to wrath: but bring them up in the nurture and admonition of the Lord" (Ephesians 6:4)

"Lo, children are an heritage of the LORD: and the fruit of the womb is his reward.

As arrows are in the hand of a mighty man; so are children of the youth. Happy is the man that hath his quiver full of them" (Psalm 127:3–5a).

"Let all bitterness, and wrath, and anger, and clamour, and evil speaking, be put away from you, with all malice: And be ye kind one to another, tenderhearted, forgiving one another, even as God for Christ's sake hath forgiven you" (Ephesians 4:31–32).

"Be ye angry, and sin not: let not the sun go down upon your wrath" (Ephesians 4:26).

STANDING FIRM IN THE WIND

Boy, it was quite windy out there today. I could hear the American flag really whipping around. That old American flag was taking a real beating out there. Even though it was fighting to keep flying, it was still standing for our country. It was still doing its job as a symbol for America.

Seeing that flag reminded me that lately I was feeling like a strong wind was tossing me about. I was feeling discouraged about a situation involving some close friends. I reached out to God and began reading in Matthew. God led me to Matthew 9 and the story of when Jesus healed the man sick with palsy. One verse in particular stood out to me, "Jesus seeing their faith said unto the sick of the palsy; Son, be of good cheer; thy sins be forgiven thee" (Matt. 9:2).

Four men carried a man they cared about upon a bed to see Jesus. They even had to break open the roof of a house and lower the man down. Because of their faith in Jesus, he forgave the man's sins and healed him so he could walk again.

Suddenly I realized I couldn't keep focusing on the people I was worried about. I have to put my faith in Jesus. I have to have faith and trust that he can fix any and every problem. He can heal the brokenhearted, the sick, and the downcast. He will forgive all our sins. There is nothing too hard for him to do. My job is to simply stand on his foundation and let him work.

Disappointments and trials whip us around like the wind. We get beaten up and tossed about. We struggle to keep standing. As long as we stay faithful to God, our testimony will still fly like our old American flag. Our faith in Jesus will show others you can be strong in the Lord and he will hold you up through the troubles that life blows your way.

"But Jesus turned him about, and when he saw her, he said, Daughter, be of good comfort; thy faith hath made thee whole. And the woman was made whole from that hour" (Matthew 9:22).

"Then touched he their eyes, saying, according to your faith be it unto you" (Matthew 9:29).

"And all things, whatsoever ye shall ask in prayer, believing, ye shall receive" (Matthew 21:22).

"Ah Lord GOD! behold, thou hast made the heaven and the earth by thy great power and stretched out arm, and there is nothing too hard for thee" (Jeremiah 32:17).

THE WARMTH OF LOVE TAKES TIME

On a busy work night, I wanted to make pulled pork for dinner, but I didn't have time to put it in the crock pot that morning. So I put it in a pan with BBQ sauce, covered it with aluminum foil, and put the oven on a low setting.

An hour later, I took it out, and I was disappointed that the pork was tough and looked dry. I thought about it for a moment and put it back in the oven just to see what would happen. A half hour later, I was thrilled to see, sure enough, my pulled pork was juicy and I was able to cut it with a fork. I just didn't give it enough time to cook at first.

After that, I was texting a friend back and forth about parenting our children when I realized, like when it comes to cooking, loving and parenting our children takes time too. Human hearts are hard and tough at first. Over time, God's love seeps in and softens them. The more we pray for those we love, the greater the work the Lord does in their lives.

Our words toward them need to not be demanding or demeaning. It takes love and kindness to win them over. Sometimes we can get impatient and want them to change right away. With that attitude, we tend to get in the way of what the Lord is doing with them. That's when we need to step back and be patient, knowing the Lord is at hand.

My mom told me my grandfather used to say when it came to cooking meat, "Low and slow is the best way." Our hearts work the same way—a little warmth coming from others and slow timing to allow God's mighty hand to work.

"A new commandment I give unto you, That ye love one another; as I have loved you, that ye also love one another. By this shall all men know that ye are my disciples, if ye have love one to another" (John 13:34–35).

"A soft answer turneth away wrath: but grievous words stir up anger" (Prov. 15:1).

"Better is the end of a thing than the beginning thereof: and the patient in spirit is better than the proud in spirit" (Ecclesiastes 7:8).

"As the Father hath loved me, so have I loved you: continue ye in my love" (John 15:9).

WHAT HAVE YOU PROVIDED?

During the month of June, schools everywhere are sending off young men and women into the world to start a new phase in their lives. For four years, schools have provided them with the knowledge and understanding they need to be successful. Behind the scenes, their parents have provided support and guidance with the hope of preparing them with all they need to face the real world.

In 1 Chronicles, King David was preparing the materials needed to build the temple for God. He knew he wasn't the one who would build the temple. His son, Solomon, was. David was gathering all that was needed so his son would not lack anything for the task. He provided tools, silver, gold, wood, and the plans, all the necessities Solomon would need.

But he didn't stop there. Once everything was gathered, he went to the Lord in prayer and asked for God to give his son a perfect heart so he would keep the Lord's commandments, testimonies, and statutes. David made this request before God so Solomon would "build the palace for which I had made provision."

That statement right there stuck out to me. David gathered the physical provisions needed for Solomon to build a house for the Lord. Then he prayed for him and asked the Lord to bless him.

As parents, we make the provisions needed for our children to live a life that would please the Lord. We provide them with the love and nurturing they need to feel secure in life. We give them the instructions and wisdom they need to be successful. After all that, we shield them with our faith and cover them with our prayers as we send them off into the world.

What better path can we start our children on then to show them the example of our own close and personal relationship with the Lord? The best foundation we can lay for them is to encourage them to personally know Jesus as their Savior. He is the one that will continue to watch over them and provide for them even when they are not within our sight.

"And give unto Solomon my son a perfect heart, to keep thy commandments, thy testimonies, and thy statutes, and to do all these things, and to build the palace, for the which I have made provision" (1 Chronicles 29:19).

"For other foundation can no man lay than that is laid, which is Jesus Christ" (1 Corinthians 3:11).

"For the LORD giveth wisdom: out of his mouth cometh knowledge and understanding. He layeth up sound wisdom for the righteous: he is a buckler to them that walk uprightly" (Proverbs 2:6–7).

"My son, forget not my law; but let thine heart keep my commandments: For length of days, and long life, and peace, shall they add to thee" (Proverbs 3:1–2).

WHAT REALLY MATTERS

Yogurt is a breakfast food. No, it's a snack food. This was an argument I had with someone years ago. We were determined to prove each other wrong. Our discussion got so heated that it led to other arguments.

Years passed, and I lost touch with the other person. As I look back on that now, I laugh as I have come to an important conclusion. Neither one of us were right or wrong. The whole argument didn't matter. When and how you choose to eat your yogurt is nothing more than a personal food preference.

What really matters is how you express your opinion and how you listen and respect the other person in the discussion. Too many people nitpick and argue about silly details that have no real value in life. Sometimes we need to just agree to disagree.

The same goes for our personal convictions on how we live our lives. Stop and think before voicing your opinion. Is the issue you want to discuss something you feel the Holy Spirit leading you to bring up? Is it Bible-based? I mean, is there clear evidence and commandments in the Bible to back up your beliefs? Is it an issue that you feel is important for the other person's safety and well-being?

Serious issues like drugs, alcohol, gambling, and adultery are some examples of need to discuss issues that may harm a person and his or her family. When you feel led to discuss these issues with someone who might need help, be cautious and tread lightly.

First, pray. Ask God to help you put aside your personal feelings so you won't get too worked up in the discussion. Pray for the other person as well. Everyone needs someone to pray for him or her. Pray that God will help the other person and guide this individual in his or her life.

Second, approach with love. Start by letting that person know you care about him or her. Show this individual you care about him or her too.

Third, back it up. If you feel a strong conviction about something, back it up with verses in the Bible. Remember, God's Word is a powerful tool to help us and guide us on how to live a blessed life. Use it. Gain evidence and biblical truth from it so, when others question you, you can give a clear answer on why you live the way you do.

Fourth and foremost, tell the other person your story. If you've "been there, done that," tell the other person about what you've experienced and what you've learned. A great way to reach someone is to show him or her how God has helped you overcome things in your life. Tell this person about God's great love for you and all he has done for you. If the person sees the change in you, this individual may want God in his or her life too.

I still like to have yogurt for breakfast, especially with fruit and cereal on top. Yum! I will always remember what I learned from my disagreement over yogurt though. I learned not to argue about things that don't really matter. Always speak with love and respect. Agree to disagree about simple preferences. Most importantly, live as a godly example for others to follow. God bless!

"Let nothing be done through strife or vainglory; but in lowliness of mind let each esteem other better than themselves" (Philippians 2:3).

"Be not deceived; God is not mocked: for whatsoever a man soweth, that shall he also reap. For he that soweth to his flesh shall of the flesh reap corruption; but he that soweth to the Spirit shall of the Spirit reap life everlasting" (Galatians 6:7–8).

"With all lowliness and meekness, with longsuffering, forbearing one another in love; Endeavouring to keep the unity of the Spirit in the bond of peace" (Ephesians 4:2–3).

"Walk in wisdom toward them that are without, redeeming the time. Let your speech be alway with grace, seasoned with salt, that ye may know how ye ought to answer every man" (Colossians 4:5–6).

WILL YOU BE THERE?

The daily devotional[7] this morning talked about Bud Paxson, the co-founder of Home Shopping Network and Pax-TV. Back in 1986, he was a very successful businessman, but his marriage was failing. He may have had wealth, but he felt bankrupt in what mattered most. On Christmas Day, his wife told him she was leaving him for another man. After that, he agreed to go with his children on a planned vacation to Las Vegas, despite his heartbreak.

In his room, he picked up a Gideon Bible and read Romans 5:8.[8] He learned that God loved him, and he put his faith and trust in Jesus as his Savior. From then on, his whole world changed. Bud said, "The moment I put my faith in Jesus Christ, an overwhelming peace came over me. I knew at that moment that God loved me."[9] Later on Bud went on to help fund Place of Hope, a home that takes in foster children and helps teens, young adults, and pregnant woman.[10]

What an amazing testimony. Imagine of all places, Las Vegas, the city of sin, where a man believed in Jesus as his Savior by reading a Gideon Bible found in a drawer in his hotel room.

My mom loved watching the Home Shopping Network. Since she was often sick and in bed, she would do all her shopping on there. I wondered if she knew Bud Paxson's story. Oh, how I wished I could share it with her and talk to her about it. Then it hit me, and I laughed as I realized that Bud Paxson and my mom are both in heaven. She can talk to him in person, and they can share their stories with each other.

It will be so wonderful when we get to heaven and see so many different people there. Our beloved family members and friends will be standing with open arms, waiting to greet us. We will get to meet famous people we read about in our history books as well as patriarchs from the Bible like Abraham, Jesus's disciples, and the apostle Paul.

---

[7] Romans 5:8, King James Bible

[8] Dr. David Jeremiah, "10 Things God Loves about You," *Turning Points*, February 9, 2017.

[9] "The Light of God's Word Lights up the Holidays," accessed October 21, 2017, http://blog.gideons.org/2010/12/lowell-paxson-pax-testimony-christmas.

[10] "Our History," accessed October 21, 2017, https://www.placeofhope.com/our-history.

Many Christians have felt the same longing in their heart. The first face they want to see is Jesus, their loving Savior. God sent Jesus, his precious Son, to earth to die on the cross as a sacrifice to pay the debt we owe for all our sins. All it takes to get into heaven is to believe in Jesus and accept his gift of salvation on the cross and invite him into our hearts. Then we are welcomed into heaven for all eternity.

Will you be there? Have you invited Jesus into your heart and accepted him as your Savior?

"But I would not have you to be ignorant, brethren, concerning them which are asleep, that ye sorrow not, even as others which have no hope. For if we believe that Jesus died and rose again, even so them also which sleep in Jesus will God bring with him" (1 Thessalonians 4:13–14).

"Then we which are alive and remain shall be caught up together with them in the clouds, to meet the Lord in the air: and so shall we ever be with the Lord. Wherefore comfort one another with these words" (1 Thessalonians 4:17–18).

"In this was manifested the love of God toward us, because that God sent his only begotten Son into the world, that we might live through him" (1 John 4:9).

WILL YOU FORGIVE ME?

How far would you go to show someone you forgive him or her? Are there any acts that you would just not forgive? A friend stands you up. Your husband forgets your anniversary. A family member betrays you or hurts you in some way. How would you ever forgive the man who killed your husband or wife?

I know the story of a woman who not only forgave the people who killed her husband but also decided to take her daughter and live with them. She even helped them take care of their families. This is the story of Elisabeth Elliot.[11]

Elisabeth's husband, Jim, was one of five missionaries who felt a great burden to bring the gospel to the Waodani Indians in Ecuador. As they were trying to speak to the Waodani people, they were speared to death. Despite her great loss, Elisabeth felt that God wanted her to forgive the people who took her husband from her. Elisabeth also discovered that, not only had God called her to forgive them, she was to also teach them about God's love for them and to continue with her husband's missionary work. Elisabeth, in her own flesh, could not grant them forgiveness, but she gave her life to Christ. Because of that, God used her to be the ultimate example of love and forgiveness toward others.

Forgiveness is so powerful. It frees the person receiving it from the guilt-caused pain. What's even more amazing though is that forgiveness also frees those who grant it from the pain and anger of being hurt. Something this great can only come from God.

When I struggle with forgiving someone, God reminds me that he has forgiven me for all the wrong things I have done. He sent his Son, Jesus, to die on the cross so he could forgive me for all my sins. Who am I to not forgive another person? Just like with Elisabeth, God is calling all of us to share his love and forgiveness with others. The best part is that we don't have to do it alone. We can do it with his help.

---

[11] "Elisabeth Elliot," www.elisabethelliot.org.

"Then Jesus said, Father forgive them, for they know not what they do" (Luke 23:34).

"And be ye kind one to another, tenderhearted, forgiving one another, even as God for Christ's sake hath forgiven you" (Ephesians 4:32).

"For thou, Lord, art good, and ready to forgive; and plenteous in mercy unto all them that call upon thee" (Psalm 86:5).

"So that contrariwise ye ought rather to forgive him, and comfort him, lest perhaps such a one should be swallowed up with overmuch sorrow" (2 Corinthians 2:7).

WITH A GIVING HEART

The Bible says, "Give and it shall be given unto you." When we give, God always gives back to us somehow. Today when people give, they say to "pay it forward." You give to someone, and he or she will in turn pass the kindness on and give to someone else. Before you know it, a chain reaction breaks out where people are giving more and more.

Over the last few years, I gave what I call the blessed fifty dollars. God would lay on my heart to donate fifty dollars to someone or some cause in need. The next thing you know, fifty dollars would come back to me through a friend, a family member, or some other unexpected source. One time, my bank sent me a check for fifty dollars, which they said they owed me from overcharging me in fees over the years. Imagine that!

Recently I learned about a different type of giving—giving love and compassion to those around you. This can be the hardest type of giving of all. You may have heard of sacrificial giving, which means you give even when it may hurt you financially to do so. That's a true test of faith. How about giving a kind word to someone who was just rude to you? Or how about giving a smile to someone you know doesn't like you? Try going the extra mile and offering to help this person in his or her time of need. This person's reaction might surprise you. He or she may even give back to you the kindness you shared with him or her.

Giving love and compassion to those who hurt you is what Jesus did on the cross. He forgave and loved those who nailed him to the cross while he was still there in pain. His testimony of love is what we can live by if we trust him as our Savior. His love through us can start the greatest chain reaction of giving the world has ever seen.

Jesus has loved us and forgiven us for all the wrong we have ever done. He gives to us with an unconditional love in his heart, and now it's time for us to pay it forward.

"And whosoever shall compel thee to go a mile, go with him twain. Give to him that asketh thee, and from him that would borrow of thee turn not thou away" (Matthew 5:41–42).

"And as ye would that men should do to you, do ye also to them likewise" (Luke 6:31).

"I have shewed you all things, how that so labouring ye ought to support the weak, and to remember the words of the Lord Jesus, how he said, It is more blessed to give than to receive" (Acts 20:35).

"Every man according as he purposeth in his heart, so let him give; not grudgingly, or of necessity: for God loveth a cheerful giver" (2 Corinthians 9:7).

"WON'T YOU BE MY NEIGHBOR?"

We all know the song and remember the sweater and tennis shoes. Mr. Rogers was a favorite character for so many children over the years. His lessons on life issues were meant to bring hope and healing through his TV show.

My son recently spoke about Mr. Rogers at his senior chapel. He mentioned that Mr. Rogers was a servant who faithfully served others through the years by teaching them.

On one of the pages in a psalms devotional book I have, I saw a quote from Fred Rogers book, *The World According to Mr. Rogers: Important Things to Know*. The quote mentioned the purpose of life is to listen to God and your neighbor and to respond by being helpful.[12]

I was recently thinking about the words of his opening song, "Won't you be my neighbor?" when something dawned on me. It reminded me of the verse in Matthew 22:39 that states, "Thou shalt love thy neighbor as thyself." I know that Fred Rogers was a minister. I wonder if he thought of that verse when he was asking all the children watching his show to be his neighbor. It seems to me that he made a commitment to love all of them and teach them. In the Bible, your neighbor is anyone around you in your life. What a blessing that is to try to reach out to so many people with the intent to love and serve them.

Only God could give us a heart full of love like that. Some of us struggle to love the person we work with or even live with, never mind love an entire national audience. But take heart! No matter what we feel inside, we are never beyond God's reach. He can change any heart and fill it with love for those around them.

God has blessed me with the ability to write devotionals so I can bring hope to others. This is something I could never do without his love and support. If someone were to ask me why I take the time to write when I may never get published or anything in return, I would simply reply, "Because I would like you to be my neighbor."

---

[12] C. A. Dallman and R. Petersen, My Daily Psalms & Prayers (Lincolnwood, Ill.: Publications International, 2010).

"Greater love hath no man than this, that a man lay down his life for his friends" (John 15:13).

"For I am persuaded, that neither death, nor life, nor angels, nor principalities, nor powers, nor things present, nor things to come, nor height, nor depth, nor any other creature, shall be able to separate us from the love of God, which is in Christ Jesus our Lord" (Romans 8:38–39).

"A new commandment I give unto you, That ye love one another; as I have loved you, that ye also love one another" (John 13:34).

"And the King shall answer and say unto them, Verily I say unto you, Inasmuch as ye have done it unto one of the least of these my brethren, ye have done it unto me" (Matthew 25:40).

WOULD YOU GIVE THEM AN UMBRELLA?

It was a cold, rainy day. I got out of the car, grabbed my bags, and ran for the overhang in front of our church door. Just before I opened the door to go inside, I paused and saw one of the ladies in my church coming out of her car. She didn't have an umbrella, and she was walking in the rain. My first thought was to go inside because it was getting windy and my hair was getting messed up. Then I realized what I needed to do, so I opened up my umbrella and walked back out into the rain. I greeted my friend and held my umbrella over the two of us as we walked back to the church door.

This seemed like such a small deed to do at first, but I later realized it represented something much bigger. God used that one random act of kindness to remind me there is another kind of umbrella I need to share with people, one that will cover them in the terrible rainstorms of life, one of comfort, love, and grace. It is an umbrella that our Lord and Savior, Jesus, gives us to shelter and protect us in this world. When we ask him to come into our hearts and accept him as our Savior, he brings us a peace that passes all understanding.

Sometimes it is hard to tell people about Jesus. We never know how they will react. They may get angry or push us away. We should think of it this way: if we knew the cure for cancer, would we share it with others? Of course, if it meant we could save their lives.

That's the way it is with telling others about Jesus. He has a cure for much more than the sicknesses and troubles of this world. He died on the cross as a sacrifice to wash away all our sins so we could be whiter than snow. We can rejoice daily knowing that our name is in the Book of Life and one day he will bring us home to heaven.

The next time you see someone struggling in life, just think, *If I saw this person out in a bad storm, would I give him or her an umbrella?* Jesus has something greater for you to give this person. He wants you to give this individual an opportunity to hear the gospel, something that will help this person through the many storms in life and bring him or her safely home to a glorious place in heaven. Be sure to always carry the gospel umbrella wherever you go. You never know who might need it.

"And he said unto them, Go ye into all the world, and preach the gospel to every creature" (Mark 16:15).

"Come now, and let us reason together, saith the Lord : though your sins be as scarlet, they shall be as white as snow; though they be red like crimson, they shall be as wool" (Isaiah 1:18).

"And how shall they preach, except they be sent? as it is written, How beautiful are the feet of them that preach the gospel of peace, and bring glad tidings of good things!" (Romans 10:15).

"And for me, that utterance may be given unto me, that I may open my mouth boldly, to make known the mystery of the gospel, For which I am an ambassador in bonds: that therein I may speak boldly, as I ought to speak" (Ephesians 6:19–20).

Y - Yourself

Yes, it is important to put Jesus first and others second, but that doesn't mean you forget about yourself. We are precious in God's sight. He loves us more than we will ever know this side of heaven. With his love, he longs to take care of us and provide for all our needs. When we ask Jesus to come into our hearts and accept him as our Savior, he invites the Holy Spirit to come along as well and dwell in us. This makes it so our bodies become the temple of the Holy Spirit. Should we not minister to ourselves and take care of this temple as an act of obedience and service to God?

God encourages us in his Word to take care of ourselves so we may be a better servant for him. May the devotions in this section encourage your heart and comfort you in God's love. May you be refreshed with his Word.

A CHANGE OF PLANS

We all have hopes and dreams along with big and small plans. The greatest plans of all are the God-inspired ones.

"Be still and know that I am God."[13] This verse is from the book of Psalms during King David's reign, way after the life of Joseph in the book of Genesis, but its meaning was portrayed in the life of Joseph.

Hated by his jealous brothers, Joseph was sold as a slave to a band of Midianites and brought down to Egypt. He found himself in the house of Potiphar, one of Pharaoh's captain of the guards. Joseph led a good life there being in charge of all Potiphar's affairs, but he wasn't meant to stay. Once again, someone meant evil against him. Potiphar's wife lusted after Joseph and tried her best to coax him into sleeping with her. Joseph's response was, "How then can I do this great wickedness and sin against God?"[14] He fled from her but was falsely accused and sent to prison.

Each time Joseph had a change for the worse taking place in his life, the Bible mentions the "Lord was with Joseph."[15] Joseph would have been content living in his father's land and serving in his family, but God had bigger plans for Joseph.

Due to circumstances beyond his control, Joseph made it through the rough seas of life, only for God to guide him to become the second-in-command to the Pharaoh of Egypt himself. Joseph interpreted a dream for Pharaoh's butler, who was in prison with him. Two years after the butler was restored to Pharaoh's service, Joseph was recommended to help Pharaoh interpret a dream and save nations of people from starving from a famine that covered the whole earth.

Joseph faced different changes in life, and each one was for a greater purpose. Joseph could also be pictured like Jesus, for Jesus also left the comfort of his Father's home in heaven, according to God's plan, to come to live upon the earth where he suffered from a hard human life and died on the cross to save the human race from death and hell.

---

[13] Psalm 46:10
[14] Genesis 39:9
[15] Genesis 39:21

Joseph saved people from physical hunger. Jesus saves us from spiritual hunger and leads us to a closer relationship with God through his gift of salvation. Don't be afraid if God leads you to make a change of plans in life. For the purpose he has for you is far greater than you can imagine.

"And the LORD was with Joseph, and he was a prosperous man; and he was in the house of his master the Egyptian. And his master saw that the LORD was with him, and that the LORD made all that he did to prosper in his hand" (Genesis 39:2–3).

"And Joseph's master took him, and put him into the prison, a place where the king's prisoners were bound: and he was there in the prison. But the LORD was with Joseph, and shewed him mercy, and gave him favour in the sight of the keeper of the prison" (Genesis 39:20–21).

"And Joseph said unto them, Fear not: for am I in the place of God? But as for you, ye thought evil against me; but God meant it unto good, to bring to pass, as it is this day, to save much people alive" (Genesis 50:19–20).

A CLEAN HEART RESOLUTION

It's a New Year! Time to make a resolution to exercise more and eat right. Time to quit smoking and eating lots of junk food. Hey, let's even make a new schedule and get to bed early and get up early.

Seize the day! Many people focus so much on bettering themselves physically that they forget that our bodies are a package deal—mind, body, and spirit. In Matthew 22:37, Jesus reminds us to "love the Lord thy God with all thy heart, and with all thy soul, and with all thy mind." Notice God mentions the heart first. If we ask Jesus to come into our heart and forgive us of our sins, he can clean out our hearts and make us whole. Once our hearts are fixed, the mind, body, and spirit will be renewed as well.

Christians are like plants. We need some important elements to survive:

A. Prayer is like water. It flows from within us through Jesus to God. What a great way to build our relationship with him.

B. The Bible is like soil. It's our foundation. It keeps us grounded and supported in our spiritual growth.

C. Church is like sunshine. It beams through us and feeds our souls. Good preaching based on the Word of God can change anyone's heart. Some plants may grow with little or even no sunshine, but they won't have a strong, fruitful, and healthy long life. Christians are no different.

Remember as you go through this New Year, if you're battling any bad habits, the mind and body will follow if you cure the heart. Let Jesus in!

"Watch and pray, that ye enter not into temptation: the spirit indeed is willing, but the flesh is week" (Matthew 26:41).

"So then faith cometh by hearing, and hearing by the word of God" (Romans 10:17).

"Thy word have I hide in mine heart, that I might not sin against thee" (Psalm 119:11).

"The grass withereth, the flower fadeth: but the word of our God shall stand forever" (Isaiah 40:8).

A GREAT REMINDER

Going to a new class for the first time can make you nervous. You never know where to sit. It's like you are in first grade all over again.

I walked into an English class my first year of college and sat toward the back. I found a seat near three guys. I remember talking to them and having class discussions with them. You know it's funny. I sat near a guy who I thought was really attractive. I also sat near a guy who was a Christian.

That Christian young man said something to me that gave me a feeling that brought more happiness, joy, and a smile on my face greater than anything any man has ever said to me or given me. It wasn't romantic or having anything to do with love. On the last day of class, we all said our good-byes, and he said to me, "Well, I'll see you in heaven someday." That, to me, is the greatest thing anyone could ever say, greater than "I love you." He reminded me of what was most important, where my main focus should be.

At the time, my focus was on being single and hoping to meet someone. It was also on bettering my life for my son and me. Instead my focus should have been on living for Jesus and trusting him with the cares of this life. What that young man said to me really put things into perspective.

We will see each other in heaven someday, where happiness will never end, where there will be no more sickness and pain. The world will pass away and the lusts thereof, but heaven, the home Jesus calls us to, will last forever.

"The grass withereth, the flower fadeth: but the word of our God shall stand for ever" (Isaiah 40:8).

"In my Father's house are many mansions: if it were not so, I would have told you. I go to prepare a place for you" (John 14:2).

"Then we which are alive and remain shall be caught up together with them in the clouds, to meet the Lord in the air: and so shall we ever be with the Lord" (1 Thessalonians 4:17).

"And God shall wipe away all tears from their eyes; and there shall be no more death, neither sorrow, nor crying, neither shall there be any more pain: for the former things are passed away. And he that sat upon the throne said, Behold, I make all things new. And he said unto me, Write: for these words are true and faithful" (Revelation 21:4–5).

A NEW YEAR, A NEW PATH

The beginning of the New Year is like standing at the foot of a path. You pause at the edge wondering what twists, bends, and hills you will face. You may have new goals you want to achieve. You may meet new people and add them to your circle of friends. A new home or change of career might be in store for you. Perhaps there will be new life added to your family with the birth of a baby.

For some people, this year will bring a much-needed second chance at a new beginning. It's out with the old year and in with the new as you look forward to what's ahead. A new year is always a precious gift from God, for it is another year to live for him.

In the beginning, you will start out strong and confident, but when the path gets tough, you may get down. Be sure to keep your head up and keep going. Yes, you may fall at times and feel discouraged, but there is hope. You can find your way to the end. You never have to travel this path alone. A hand is always reaching down to pick you up.

You have a loving Savior and God. Jesus will provide for you. He will always give you what you need to endure until the end. Don't be afraid to let go and let him completely take over and carry you. It will be his pleasure to do so. He will protect you. He will comfort you in time of need and lift you up. Even when things are going great, he is there by your side to share in your joy.

And as you journey down this path of a new year together, God will be sure to invite friends and family to stand along the side to cheer you on and pray for you all the way.

"Thy word is a lamp unto my feet, and a light unto my path" (Psalm 119:105).

"The Lord is my light and my salvation; whom shall I fear? the Lord is the strength of my life; of whom shall I be afraid?" (Psalm 27:1).

"The Lord is my strength and my shield; my heart trusted in him, and I am helped: therefore my heart greatly rejoiceth; and with my song will I praise him" (Psalm 28:7).

"Trust in the Lord with all thine heart; and lean not unto thine own understanding. In all thy ways acknowledge him, and he shall direct thy paths" (Proverbs 3:5–6).

A PUMPKIN HEART

In a world where death and destruction are all around us, we must remember to guard our hearts. Before we can guard our hearts, we must do something first. For guarding a heart that is left unclean is like guarding a fort with the enemy already inside.

The first step is to clean it out.

"How?" you might ask.

This can only be done by the cleansing blood of Jesus. Jesus came to earth to die on the cross and pay the penalty for all our sins. If he didn't pay the penalty for us, then our hearts would be left full of sin. Our sins separate us from God for all eternity.

Picture it like carving a pumpkin.[16] Inside of the pumpkin is a lot of seeds and pulp. It's funny to watch children squeal and say "Eww!" when you pull out all the gross stuff. Then once the pumpkin is cleaned out, the carving begins. A simple pumpkin can be turned into a beautiful work of art. How amazing it is that the process is also used on us as people.

Jesus comes along and knocks on the door of our hearts. When we say yes to him as our Savior, he then comes in, cleans out all the bad sin, and shines his light through us. We too become a work of art in God's hands.

Hatred is melted, and love is put in its place. Depression is lifted, and joy is felt. Anger is gone, and forgiveness is freely given. Oh, how the love of God can change anyone.

As you pass by a pumpkin, may it remind you of what Jesus did for you on the cross. Then ask yourself this question, "Will I invite him in?"

---

[16] Liz Curtis Higgs and Nancy Munger, *The Pumpkin Patch Parable* (Tommy Nelson, 2010).

"But if we walk in the light, as he is in the light, we have fellowship one with another, and the blood of Jesus Christ his Son cleanseth us from all sin" (1 John 1:7).

"The heart is deceitful above all things, and desperately wicked: who can know it?" (Jeremiah 17:9).

"Keep thy heart with all diligence; for out of it are the issues of life" (Proverbs 4:23).

"For God sent not his Son into the world to condemn the world; but that the world through him might be saved" (John 3:17).

ALWAYS REJOICE

The engine light comes on. You immediately start calculating how much money you have in the bank. You worry how you will get to work if something serious is wrong with the car.

More bills are coming in than you have income to cover it all. Either you or a close family member was just diagnosed with a serious illness. Whether it be financial trouble, illness, prodigal children, or a lost relationship with a spouse, we all face the hardest of times that seem to come crashing down upon us.

What does the Bible say to do? Rejoice always. Say what? Yes, rejoice. How? Rejoice that God is still sovereign. Rejoice that he is all powerful and he is on the throne. Praise him that his hand is not short. He can and will hear your prayers, provide for your needs, and reach down to you and comfort you in all your trials and tribulations. He will walk with you through all that you face. "I am with you always," he promises in Matthew 28:20.

Paul and Silas were stripped of their clothing, beaten, and thrown in prison for preaching the gospel and telling people about Jesus. Even though they were doing what was right, they were punished for it. How did they respond? They remembered to rejoice. They knew God was with them. His hand was on their lives, and so they sang praises to God at midnight. As a result of their rejoicing and faithfulness to him, God caused an earthquake to open the doors of the prison. It scared the prison guard so much he got on his knees and asked, "Sirs, what must I do to be saved?" Paul told him, "Believe on the Lord Jesus Christ and thou shalt be saved."

That is what we need to do, to believe on the Lord Jesus Christ. Believe he is the Son of God. Believe he came to die on the cross for our sins and trust him as our Savior and invite him into our hearts.

Paul and Silas were released from prison that night. But the greater victory was the fact that they were freed from a stronger prison, the same prison we all face, the prison of focusing our hearts and minds on our bad situation instead of focusing on the one who can help us, Jesus.

No matter what you are facing in your life right now, take a moment to rejoice in the Lord who is mighty and true. Remember this world is not our home. We're just passing through.[17] A greater place is waiting for you.

---

[17] Jim Reeves, "This World Is Not My Home."

"Teaching them to observe all things whatsoever I have commanded you: and, lo, I am with you alway, even unto the end of the world. Amen" (Matthew 28:20).

"Rejoice in the Lord alway: and again I say, Rejoice. Let your moderation be known unto all men. The Lord is at hand" (Philippians 4:4).

"And suddenly there was a great earthquake, so that the foundations of the prison were shaken: and immediately all the doors were opened, and every one's bands were loosed" (Acts 16:26).

"And brought them out, and said, Sirs, what must I do to be saved? And they said, Believe on the Lord Jesus Christ, and thou shalt be saved, and thy house" (Acts 16:30–31).

BEWARE OF ENTICERS

Couponing is my new favorite hobby! I gather flyers from various places and sit for hours cutting coupons. I've gotten pretty good at matching coupons with sales so I can get the best deals. It gives you such a rush when you find an amazing deal and save a lot of money.

This past week, I noticed couponing is starting to become a little bit of an obsession. I think about sales and coupons all the time. I have even gone a little overboard with stocking up on things. I soon realized I started going over my weekly budget because I was afraid I would miss out on a good deal if I didn't buy something right away. My living room and kitchen had piles of flyers everywhere. My son warned me not to go crazy with this new passion. There is nothing wrong with couponing to save money, but if it spills into other areas of your life, then you have a problem.

God has taught me that this is how enticers work. An enticer is something that intrigues you and pulls you into a zone that takes all of your focus. The most innocent activities turn into enticers, which lead to addictions or unhealthy obsessions.

Enticers come in many forms. The danger comes when we start to let go of our priorities such as family, health, and our relationship with God. Think about the activities in your life. What takes away most of your attention? Is it a dynamic career that requires you to work fifty-plus hours a week? Perhaps it's surfing the internet all hours of the night or playing video games all weekend long.

Beware of destructive enticers such as alcohol, drugs, gambling, and pornography. They make you feel the excitement you desire in life but then leave you in a ditch you can't crawl out of. It is important to understand that harmful addictions will always leave you wanting more and never leave you satisfied.

If an enticer is taking you away from spending time with your family, causing you to lose many hours of sleep, and, most importantly, taking you away from Bible reading, prayer, and going to church, it may be time to say good-bye to it. Stop and think, *Do I have control over this, or does it have control over me?*

Moderation is the key to a healthy life. A little of something is far more enjoyable than too much. We need to learn to balance things in life. My number-one priority is my relationship with Jesus. He provides all I need, so my day starts and ends with Bible reading and prayer. My second priority is my family and my home, which come before work and hobbies. Having a set schedule each week helps me to give each area of my life the attention it deserves.

I still love couponing, but I limit it to only one afternoon a week and no more than that.

"And be not conformed to this world: but be ye transformed by the renewing of your mind, that ye may prove what is that good, and acceptable, and perfect will of God" (Romans 12:2).

"Set your affection on things above, not on things on the earth" (Colossians 3:2).

"Flee also youthful lusts: but follow righteousness, faith, charity, peace, with them that call on the Lord out of a pure heart" (2 Timothy 2:22).

"Be not overcome of evil, but overcome evil with good" (Romans 12:21).

DESIRING MARRIAGE

God has instilled in us a great desire to find that special someone to share our lives with. For some, that desire is never fulfilled but changed into a desire to serve the Lord and others more. For the rest, that desire is still there, waiting to be fulfilled in the right way. If you rush into things or fail to meet the requirements God has placed upon you, your marriage can end in failure. This is something no one wants. There are steps you can take to make sure that doesn't happen.

First, wait upon the Lord, and trust in him. When the desire for marriage becomes so great that you feel lonely and depressed, surrender it to God. Let him know all that's going on inside you. He cares for you and wants you to have a blessed life. He has someone special picked out just for you, and he will bring the two of you together in his perfect timing. God is the best matchmaker. He has been in the business of matchmaking for many years.

Trust me. He doesn't need your help. He needs your devotion to him. Focusing on a closer, stronger relationship with God can help you see clearly the plan he has in place for you. It can also help lessen the strong emotions that keep you in bondage to loneliness.

Second, prepare yourself for marriage. If you were to take a long plane ride to a faraway destination, would you want the pilot to wait until he sits in the seat before he learns how to fly the plane? The same is with marriage. If you wait until your wedding day to learn how to be a good spouse, you're in for a rough ride. Learn all you can now. There are many books and messages from some great pastors that teach you from the Bible how to have a good marriage and how to understand your spouse. Talk to those who've been there and who have a good strong marriage. Learn all you can from them.

Third, look at the big picture. Hollywood does a great job of making marriage look like one big romance scene. Yes, there can be romance, but there needs to be a deeper, stronger love that is involved. I've heard from different friends that marriage was the hardest thing they've ever done. It does take a lot of work and effort from both husband and wife. Start developing the qualities that you will need to have a successful marriage, for example, learning to communicate, properly manage your finances, and put others and their needs before yourself.

Fourth, make yourself available in the right way. Quite a few dating sites and apps out there supposedly make it easier to find that special someone. Personally, I have a hard time choosing what I want on the menu at McDonald's, so the idea of looking at people's profiles and hoping to pick the right person just seems overwhelming to me.

Remember, God is the best matchmaker there is. A better choice would be to make yourself available by participating in healthy and godly activities. Church groups and mission trips would be a good place to start. Take up a healthy hobby or join a running or hiking group. The best way to meet someone is to meet him or her when you are doing something you enjoy and serving the Lord.

On the day you become man and wife, the real adventure begins. God gave us such a precious gift called marriage. A good marriage takes three people—husband, wife, and the Lord Jesus Christ—to oversee it all. Even if you find that special someone, make sure you remember our first love relationship should always be with the Lord. For only his love can truly enrich every marriage in life.

"Delight thyself also in the LORD; and he shall give thee the desires of thine heart. Commit thy way unto the LORD; trust also in him; and he shall bring it to pass" (Psalm 37:4–5).

"Wives, submit yourselves unto your own husbands, as unto the Lord" (Ephesians 5:22).

"Husbands, love your wives, even as Christ also loved the church, and gave himself for it" (Ephesians 5:25).

"For this cause shall a man leave his father and mother, and shall be joined unto his wife, and they two shall be one flesh" (Ephesians 5:31).

DO YOU LOVE GOD
MORE THAN THESE?

YouTube, Facebook, shopping, cupcakes, and cookies, and TV. What do all of these have in common? Believe it or not, each of these items can become addictions. Yes, an addiction, something you can't enjoy just a little bit of. It becomes an obsession, something you can't go a certain number of days or even hours without. You have to have it.

Obesity has been a known problem in the United States for some time now. It's easy to see how desserts can become a food addiction, but what about the rest of the list? Well, people who have a shopping addiction can easily spend eight hours a day online or shopping in stores.[18] Some people ring up over $40,000 in credit card debt just for impulse shopping. A shopping addiction can be just as bad as a gambling addiction and have some of the same consequences and effects on your family.

Americans can spend around ten hours a day on screen time.[19] This can include using smartphones, tablets, or computers. Or it could include watching YouTube, spending time on Facebook, and even watching television. There is a tremendous increase in screen addiction among children and teens today. Screen addictions are very real. I remember a time when my son used to get mad at me and feel neglected because I was texting on my phone more than I should have been. Once I realized what I was doing, I made sure I put him before my phone.

So how do you know if you have an addiction? Put it to the test. Pick something that you think may be an addiction and try going four weeks without it. If you find you can't make it that long, you may have an addiction. For some people, it isn't so much an addiction but an idol.

God warned the Israelites in the Old Testament to beware of idols. Idols take us away from spending time with God and fully becoming what he wants us to be.

---

[18] "God's Beautiful Design for Women, Day 16," accessed February 28, 2017, https://www.reviveourhearts.com/radio/revive-our-hearts/gods-beautiful-design-women-day-16.
[19] "Americans Devote More than 10 Hours a Day on Screens," accessed February 28, 2017, https://www.cnn.com/2016/06/30/health/americans-screen-time-nielsen/index.html.

How many times have you felt you should spend time reading your Bible and praying but instead get distracted by something that leads you astray? Could that something be an idol in your life?

Each year, Ash Wednesday is considered the first day of Lent. Lent signifies the forty days that Jesus wandered in the desert and fasted. Imagine forty days without food or water. I wonder if he spent the whole time praying and drawing strength from God, his heavenly Father. Those who participate in Lent usually pick one item of food to abstain from for forty days. To be honest, their dedication gave me an idea.

I admit cupcakes and cookies, among other sweets, are my weakness. I couldn't imagine giving them up. That was until I heard God's still, small voice say, "Would you do it for me?" That got my attention.

I answered him, "Yes, Lord. I would do it for you."

So for the month of March, I have decided to give up desserts, especially my favorite sweets. I know it won't be easy, but I want God to know he means more to me than the things of this world. I'm sure my body will thank me for this as well.

God has taught me, in order to overcome desires for certain things, we need to fill that desire with something from him. Pick up the Bible and get into the Word. Start praying as soon as you feel that desire come on and distract your mind by praying for people you know. Try praising God and acknowledging past blessings he has given you. Most importantly, memorize and quote scripture. Hide his Word in your heart so it will be there when you need it most (Ps. 119:11). God can help us overcome any desire we have by filling us with his love and grace. Over time, you will feel closer in your relationship with him and less chained by the things of this earth. What greater freedom could there possibly be in life?

Are you willing to take this challenge as well?

"Jesus said unto him, Thou shalt love the Lord thy God with all thy heart, and with all thy soul, and with all thy mind. This is the first and great commandment" (Matthew 22:36–37).

"Turn ye not unto idols, nor make to yourselves molten gods: I am the LORD your God" (Leviticus 19:4).

"Ye are of God, little children, and have overcome them: because greater is he that is in you, than he that is in the world" (1 John 4:4).

"So when they had dined, Jesus saith to Simon Peter, Simon, son of Jonas, lovest thou me more than these? He saith unto him, Yea, Lord; thou knowest that I love thee. He saith unto him, Feed my lambs" (John 21:15).

EMBRACING THE BARRIERS

It was one of those mornings where I felt like I would never get to work. I raced around the house grabbing all I needed for the day, hoping not to forget anything. Of course something always seems to slip my mind. I thanked God when I could finally get in the car. Just accomplishing that alone was a miracle.

As I was driving down the road, a slow driver ended up in front of me. Why is it on the days when you feel rushed there seems to be someone in front of you going as slow as possible? Instead of being grateful he was a safe driver and going the speed limit, I was praying he would just turn off somewhere.

That's when the Lord spoke to me and told me to relax and take a breath. He reminded me that sometimes barriers are put in place as an opportunity for us to stop and think. It's a moment to take that time to slow down and give yourself a chance to be at peace.

God allows things to get in our way so we can remember to take our mind off what we are doing and check in with him. If we are speeding along in life, we could be heading in the wrong direction or even heading toward danger. He slows us down so we can see if we are still in his will and to make sure our focus is on him and not on the world.

Coming up against a barrier is the perfect opportunity to draw closer to our precious Savior, to reconnect with him in a loving relationship and rest in his strong embrace.

He also gives us these precious moments to reflect on the beauty of his creation and to be reminded of the blessings he gives us. Only then do we see all that he does for us and know who he is in our lives.

Now I embrace these moments as I'm driving and catch a glimpse of the beautiful flowers and plants he created. It's a perfect time to thank him for his love, for who he is and for always answering my prayers. By the time the driver in front of me is gone, I feel refreshed and refocused.

The next time you come across a barrier in life that seems to slow you down, embrace it. God may be using it as a time to redirect your attention to him.

"Rest in the LORD, and wait patiently for him: fret not thyself because of him who prospereth in his way, because of the man who bringeth wicked devices to pass" (Psalm 37:7).

"Bless the Lord, O my soul: and all that is within me, bless his holy name" (Psalm 103:1).

"Draw nigh to God, and he will draw nigh to you. Cleanse your hands, ye sinners; and purify your hearts, ye double minded" (James 4:8).

"Come unto me, all ye that labour and are heavy laden, and I will give you rest" (Matthew 11:28).

EXERCISE YOUR FAITH

Faith is a precious gift from God. It carries us through hard times. It helps us lift up friends who are down. It shows proof of God's love shining in us. Exercising faith can be a powerful experience for those who allow it to flow through them.

Faith isn't something we get on our own. God gives it to us with the help of the Holy Spirit. By faith, we believe Jesus died on the cross for our sins and accept him as our personal Savior.

With the help of faith, Jesus said we can move mountains. For some of us, those mountains are relationship troubles, demanding jobs, problems at home, and financial hardship. Faith in the Lord can help us with all of these things. Our faith needs to be grounded in the Lord Jesus in order to work. He is the mediator between us and God. We certainly can't have faith in ourselves or others since we are all imperfect sinners.

In order for our faith to grow, it needs to be exercised. Faith is not based on feelings. Feelings are of the flesh. If we exercise our faith, good feelings will follow. If a person decided that he or she was going to walk every day but waited to feel good about it before he or she even got started, this person would never get out there. No one feels good about exercising until he or she actually does it. For some people, they don't feel good until after they're done. Once they get into a routine, it's amazing how it changes their life.

The same principle works for faith. We may not feel like reading our Bible, going to church, praying, or serving God, but if we make an effort to start and stay committed, we will feel good about it. We will have an amazing transformation take place as well as see great blessings in our lives.

The Bible is filled with stories of how God blessed those who put their faith and trust in him. Hebrews 11 tells us about many of these stories. There is nothing our God can't do for us. We just need to put our faith and trust in him. Exercise your faith in God and see how much it will grow.

"Now faith is the substance of things hoped for, the evidence of things not seen" (Hebrews 11:1).

"And the apostles said unto the Lord, Increase our faith. And the Lord said, If ye had faith as a grain of mustard seed, ye might say unto this sycamine tree, Be thou plucked up by the root, and be thou planted in the sea; and it should obey you" (Luke 17:5–6).

"And he said unto her, Daughter, be of good comfort: thy faith hath made thee whole; go in peace" (Luke 8:48).

"But without faith it is impossible to please him: for he that cometh to God must believe that he is, and that he is a rewarder of them that diligently see him" (Hebrews 11:6).

FIGHTING THE WIND

Did you ever notice the day after we have a lot of rain it's very windy? Today is one of those days. I looked out my office window and noticed a white seagull fighting against the wind. It seemed to stop after a while and just glide as the strong breeze flowed under its wings and held it up. The more I watched the majestic bird in flight, the more I realized that bird is going to have very strong muscles after all that work.

What a perfect example for me to learn from on a day like today. It just happens to be one of those days where I feel like I am fighting the wind. Some people like to call it swimming upstream. No matter how hard I try to do things right, something goes wrong.

Even on days like this, God's grace is upon me. God has taught me about faith and how it is sometimes through the trials we face in life that our faith will grow. We may not see past the trouble we are facing, but we can be assured that, in the end, God has all things in his hands. He says in his Word that he will work all things out for good and his greater purpose.[20]

What a comfort to know that he is always with us. He watches over us and is ready to help us stand. As a loving Father, he also knows when we need to exercise our faith by facing the troubles in our life. Picture a young child learning to walk for the first time. Unless you let go and let the child struggle to his or her feet on his or her own by working the muscles in his or her legs, the child will never be able to take the strong steps needed to learn to walk.

It is like that with our faith in God. Faith means trusting in him when we can't see past our troubles. Faith is believing he is there as we feel the winds of adversity blow all around us. Some days we need to just stand with our wings spread out and say, "Let it blow, Lord, for I know you are with me, strengthening me, guiding me, and making me strong."

---

[20] Romans 8:28 (KJV)

"That the trial of your faith, being much more precious than of gold that perisheth, though it be tried with fire, might be found unto praise and honour and glory at the appearing of Jesus Christ" (1 Peter 1:7).

"But the God of all grace, who hath called us unto his eternal glory by Christ Jesus, after that ye have suffered a while, make you perfect, stablish, strengthen, settle you" (1 Peter 5:10).

"And suddenly there came a sound from heaven as of a rushing mighty wind, and it filled all the house where they were sitting. And there appeared unto them cloven tongues like as of fire, and it sat upon each of them" (Acts 2:2–3).

"Therefore we are always confident, knowing that, whilst we are at home in the body, we are absent from the Lord:(For we walk by faith, not by sight:) We are confident, I say, and willing rather to be absent from the body, and to be present with the Lord" (2 Corinthians 5:6–8).

GIVE YOUR ALL TO GOD

There are many stories of fascinating people in the Bible—tales of Abraham, Moses, Esther, Ruth, and so on. Some take up whole books in the Bible to tell them.

One story has always stood out to me among the rest. It is the account of the widow and her two mites. This story is quite short. In fact, it's only about four verses long. Yet pastors all over the world has preached this story many times.

The widow in the story wasn't anyone special. Her name isn't even mentioned. She didn't have a big exciting story like Esther or Ruth. She didn't give birth to anyone famous like John the Baptist or Jesus. She was just a lowly widow who decided one day to cast in all she had, two small mites (about four cents), into the temple treasury. Little did she know, her small act of dedication and worship did not go unnoticed. Her loving Savior and creator, Jesus was sitting at the temple watching her. He thought so highly of her sacrifice, for it was all her money. To him, it was greater than the large sums of money that the rich men gave. Jesus said, "For all they did cast in of their abundance; but she of her want did cast in all that she had, even all her living."[21]

Imagine what great faith she had to give all she had to God and to trust him to provide for all her needs.

"Is your all on the altar?"[22] as the song goes? This poor widow's was. As a result, her story is written in the Word of God for millions of people to read. Her story is preached about everywhere and used by God as an example for how we should live. What a great honor for her in exchange for the small sum of her living.

This woman really gave more than she realized, for she surrendered her life into God's hands and gave with all her heart. Will you give your all to Jesus? Your time, your money, and your life?

If you do, there will be an abundance of blessings and an amazing life ahead of you. Just think, God may use your story to touch the lives of those around you, just like the story of the widow and her two mites.

---

[21] "And he called unto him his disciples, and saith unto them, Verily I say unto you, That this poor widow hath cast more in, than all they which have cast into the treasury: For all they did cast in of their abundance; but she of her want did cast in all that she had, even all her living" (Mark 12:43–44).

[22] "Is Your All on the Altar?" https://www.youtube.com/watch?v=DkD-XK9BAEs.

"Let your light so shine before men, that they may see your good works, and glorify your Father which is in heaven" (Matthew 5:15).

"Give, and it shall be given unto you; good measure, pressed down, and shaken together, and running over, shall men give into your bosom. For with the same measure that ye mete withal it shall be measured to you again" (Luke 6:38).

HOW FIRM IS YOUR FOUNDATION?

Yesterday morning I woke up to the whirlwind adventure of my son being sick and trying to head off to church to keep my commitment to teach Sunday school. Later I returned home feeling dizzy and having bad stomach pains. There was no time to rest as my overwhelming to-do list and dirty house screamed for my attention. That all had to be put aside for a last-minute run to the ER as my son could not walk because of foot pain.

While I was using the ER early check-in on the iPad—a great idea from the hospital by the way—my cat so kindly let me know she needed my attention by vomiting on the hallway stairs. Needless to say, that had to be put off for the time being—sorry, kitty—as we whisked off to the ER.

One sprained foot (a soccer injury from the day before) and two crutches later, we were home, and I was back to cleaning up my cat's little gift that she left me. I even managed to take out the overflowing trash and change the burnt-out light bulb in my headlight … with a little help of course.

Where was God in all of this? He helped me keep my composure, made me laugh when I needed it most, gave me a clear mind to think with, and helped me feel an overwhelming sense of peace through it all.

When storms come in life, you have to be sure to build a strong foundation ahead of time. Jesus mentioned in Matthew 7 that, if we hear his sayings and do them, we are like a wise man who built his house upon a rock. If we read our Bible and pray every day, we are building a firm foundation to stand upon. We are showing God that we are putting him first in life. We are also building our faith and trust in Him. If we don't do these things and wait until there is a crisis to reach out to God, we will definitely be on shaky ground. We will not have the strength or faith to face what we might be going through.

Although it may seem like my son and I went through a lot this past Sunday, to me, it seemed like an annoying rainstorm that lasted all day. God still gave me the peace and guidance to get through it all. The real test of my faith-built foundation came when my mom passed away suddenly. To be honest, during that time, I also felt an overwhelming sense of peace and was able to handle things with grace. I know my sure foundation in Jesus made it all possible.

How firm is your foundation? Will you be able to handle the storms in life? My advice to you is to start building your house upon a rock now, the rock of Jesus.

"Thou wilt keep him in perfect peace, whose mind is stayed on thee: because he trusteth in thee" (Isaiah 26:3).

"Heal me, O Lord, and I shall be healed; save me, and I shall be saved: for thou art my praise" (Jeremiah 17:14).

"Therefore whosoever heareth these sayings of mine, and doeth them, I will liken him unto a wise man, which built his house upon a rock: And the rain descended, and the floods came, and the winds blew, and beat upon that house; and it fell not: for it was founded upon a rock" (Matthew 7:24–25).

HUMBLING YOUR PRIDE

King David[23] started as a shepherd, one of the lowliest jobs. He then was a servant to King Saul and played the harp for him. He was on top of his game with a great victory over Goliath and becoming a soldier for Saul. He was then brought low running for his life as Saul became jealous of him and tried to kill him. While all this took place, David knew he was going to be king of Israel as God anointed him to be. He didn't storm the palace with pride and tell Saul he was replacing him. He waited patiently and respected Saul, even though Saul tried to kill him. David humbled himself and waited until Saul's time of ruling was over.

Jesus did something similar. He is the creator of the heavens and the earth, yet he humbled himself to become man in the flesh. He lived among us as a servant and sacrificed himself on the cross for our sakes. He didn't come storming down to the earth demanding worship. Even now he still waits patiently with his arms open and invites us to come to him and trust him as our Savior.

Pride is the foundation of all evil. The exalting of one's self to bring others low dooms you to the result of failure. For even the mightiest kingdoms in ancient history were brought down and destroyed.

Humbling one's self to lift up the Lord Jesus and esteem others will help you achieve the greatest purpose in life. The result will be a lifetime of joy and spiritual success.

Oh Lord, let me be a faithful servant to thee. May your love shine through me for all the world to see.

---

[23] 1 Samuel 16:6–1 Samuel 24

"But made himself of no reputation, and took upon him the form of a servant, and was made in the likeness of men: And being found in fashion as a man, he humbled himself, and became obedient unto death, even the death of the cross" (Philippians 2:7–8).

"Humble yourselves therefore under the mighty hand of God, that he may exalt you in due time" (1 Peter 5:6).

"And whosoever shall exalt himself shall be abased; and he that shall humble himself shall be exalted" (Matthew 23:11).

"Put on therefore, as the elect of God, holy and beloved, bowels of mercies, kindness, humbleness of mind, meekness, longsuffering" (Colosians 3:12).

KEEP YOUR FOCUS

It was an overwhelmingly stressful week. The to-do list was a mile long, my laundry and dishes were piled high, and no matter how many times I went over my finances, I was still coming up short for the month. All I could do was stop and ask, "God, why is this happening? What is going on?"

My answer was simple: I lost my focus. Instead of focusing on living for Jesus and drawing close to him, I was focusing on all my financial and worldly problems and how I could fix things. At the same time, my son had the misfortune of asking if he could go to his school track meet and his friend's house when I was at the peak of my stress. My response to him wasn't very kind.

Instead of focusing on being there for his needs, being proud of him for supporting his school team, and knowing he needed to say good-bye to his friend, who was leaving to go back to Korea, I was focusing on how many miles I would have to drive and how we were both going in two different directions.

When we lose our focus, the busy things in life take over. God warns us in the Bible not to focus on money. He said we can't serve him and money. We will hate the one and love the other. God will always provide for our needs. Sometimes he blesses us in the most miraculous way. Why would anyone want to miss out on that?

God also tells us not to worry about the cares of this world but to focus on him. We could be here today and gone tomorrow. My personal goal should be to make every day count and live life putting God and my son before everything else. When God comes first, everything else falls into place. As a parent, it is important to take every opportunity to see all the great character qualities my son is developing.

Just like a little child who clutches his favorite toy tightly in his hands, we hold on tight to the stress and worries of this world, refusing to let go. That's when the cares of this world become more than we can bear and God steps in and reminds us that we need to hand our cares over to him. He also has to gently tell us, "Remember, you're here to serve and honor me. Don't lose your focus."

"Casting all your care upon him; for he careth for you" (1 Peter 5:7).

"No servant can serve two masters: for either he will hate the one, and love the other; or else he will hold to the one, and despise the other. Ye cannot serve God and mammon (money, wealth)" (Luke 16:13).

"But seek ye first the kingdom of God, and his righteousness; and all these things shall be added unto you. Take therefore no thought for the morrow: for the morrow shall take thought for the things of itself. Sufficient unto the day is the evil thereof" (Matthew 6:33–34).

LOOK AT ME, THE REAL ME

Growing up, I, like so many other young ladies, had an issue with weight. I was not happy with my own image. I struggled to look good to everyone around me and to myself as well. I felt that, because of what I looked like, no one would ever love me. People made fun of me in school. Guys weren't asking me out.

Let me guess. The image you have right now in your mind is that I was overweight. To be honest, I weighed ninety-eight pounds my senior year in high school. Surprised? I bet you're thinking that doesn't sound like a problem. To me, it was. I was underweight and picked on for it. I felt ugly and unwanted.

Many women have had issues with their body image growing up. Having an issue with weight can be because of being overweight or underweight. Some feel they are just not attractive at all. The real issue is that we are not happy with ourselves and the world seems to sense that and feed on it.

You can look like a perfect supermodel, and someone somewhere will come along and pick out all your faults. The good news is the image on the outside doesn't matter as much as the image on the inside.

What is the image on the inside? Well, look at how you feel about yourself and your life overall. Do you feel good about who you are as a person, your career, and your relationship with your family? If not, it could be because there's something missing.

There is a reason for feeling the way you do. Let's go back to the beginning of time. When Adam and Eve sinned and were cast out of the garden of Eden, they were separated from God. They lost that personal connection with the one who created them and loved them. If you don't have that personal connection, you start to look for it in the people around you. You start to feel that, if you don't have a husband, close friends, or a big family, then you haven't fulfilled your purpose in life.

It's sad to say even people who have all that can still feel unfulfilled. That's not the answer. The answer is you need a personal relationship with the one who created you and loves you more than any person on the face of the earth. Because you are born from the line of Adam and Eve, you too suffer from the same separation from God. The only way to get that connection back is through belief in Jesus as your personal Savior and Lord. He loves you no matter what you look like on the outside. You are one of his precious children.

Once we accept Jesus as our Savior, we need to keep up with our end of the relationship. We do that by reading our Bible, going to church, and praying to him every day. We need to show him we love him because he first loved us.

Give it a try. I bet you will start to notice a change in you that is both exciting and peaceful at the same time. If you want to be satisfied with yourself, you need to forget about yourself and focus on Jesus first. He is the one who sees you as the beauty he created you to be.

When people look at me now, I often pray, "Don't let them see me, Jesus. Let them see you. You are my beauty." Let your faith in Jesus make you shine before others. They will then see the real you, a beauty in the eyes of the Lord.

"We love him, because he first loved us" (1 John 4:19).

"Give unto the LORD the glory due unto his name: bring an offering, and come before him: worship the LORD in the beauty of holiness" (1 Chronicles 16:29).

"One thing have I desired of the LORD, that will I seek after; that I may dwell in the house of the LORD all they days of my life, to behold the beauty of the LORD, and to enquire in his temple" (Psalm 27:4).

"Favor is deceitful, and beauty is vain: but a woman that feareth the LORD, she shall be praised" (Proverbs 31:30).

MY WALK WITH GOD

There is nothing like going on long walks, especially along trails near the river. It's even better going on a long walk with a friend. I get the exercise I need, I have a great conversation, and I get a chance to look at all the beautiful plants and wildlife God created.

Lately I have been feeling exhausted and out of it. I know part of it is because I haven't been out for a walk in a while. When I don't keep up with exercise, I tend to feel weak and more tired. Sometimes it's hard to get back into it. I have to give myself a push and force myself to get out there, no matter how drained I feel. I know, once I start walking again, I will feel better.

Occasionally I will go out for a quick walk by myself around the neighborhood. I call it my walk with God. I pour my heart out to him and tell him about everything going on in my life.

I haven't been doing that as much as I should. I have been trying to solve my problems myself. Needless to say, once again I got myself into a tough situation and couldn't get myself out. I was expecting God to help me and trusting him to rescue me, but I forgot to ask for his help and walk closely with him.

In the Christian faith, when we lose our close relationship with God, we do what's called "backsliding." We come so far in our close walk with the Lord but then slide back into the world.

Picture it like a child walking with his dad. They're holding hands and talking and laughing together. Next thing you know, the child sees something that catches his eye. He lets go of his father's hand and wanders a little ways, feeling confident his dad is still there. Suddenly he realizes where he is, and knowing he's gone too far, he turns around but can't find his way back to his dad. He starts to cry out in a panic. His dad gently approaches him and tells him it's okay. He kept his eye on him the whole time. He just needed him to learn his lesson. He tells him as he lovingly comforts him, "You should have stayed by my side, and then we could have looked at things together."

This is how it is when we are walking with our heavenly Father. We are at peace and confident when we are in a close relationship with him. We have a firm foundation to stand on when we read our Bible regularly, pray, and listen to his Word being preached at church.

Before long, something in the world will catch our eye and take our focus off our relationship with God. It could be anything from a hobby we enjoy to a problem we are facing, like financial trouble.

That's what my problem was. I was too focused on the financial burdens I was facing this month and forgot to stay close by God's side so we could get through everything together.

It's so important to keep walking with the Lord and comforting to know he will always hold our hand. Once I got back in a close relationship with him, not only did he teach me what I needed to learn, he also gave me a financial miracle because he is so loving and kind.

"For the LORD thy God hath blessed thee in all the works of thy hand: he knoweth thy walking through this great wilderness: these forty years the LORD thy God hath been with thee; thou hast lacked nothing" (Deuteronomy 2:7).

"The LORD is my shepherd; I shall not want. He maketh me to lie down in green pastures: he leadeth me beside the still waters" (Psalm 23:1–2).

"Ye shall walk in all the ways which the LORD your God hath commanded you, that ye may live, and that it may be well with you, and that ye may prolong your days in the land which ye shall possess" (Deuteronomy 5:33).

"He hath shewed thee, O man, what is good; and what doth the LORD require of thee, but to do justly, and to love mercy, and to walk humbly with thy God?" (Micah 6:8).

PANIC MODE

A mom waiting to pick up her son after elementary school sees that he's not there. She gets nervous as she walks into the school and asks the office where he is. She starts to panic as she hears that he took the bus home. After a quick prayer, she makes a phone call, and relief fills her after talking to his friend's mom. Her son was safely waiting at their house since no one was home.

Your car rolls to a stop as you wait for the car in front of you to move. They are kindly waiting for a pedestrian to pass by. Suddenly your car is jolted forward. You've been hit from behind. Your neck hurts, you feel nauseous, and a million thoughts run through your mind. *How bad am I hurt? How much damage? How will I get through this?* Despite your situation, an overwhelming sense of peace fills you as comforting Bible verses fill your mind.

How often do we find ourselves hitting panic mode when a stressful situation arises? Whether it's a minor problem like losing an important piece of paper or a major life change, like losing a loved one, we often react with a feeling of panic and fear.

Yesterday I booked a reservation for my son and me to go on our annual ski trip in February. I was so surprised to get such a great deal on the room that I didn't realize I had made a terrible mistake. As I checked my bank account this evening, I saw the hotel had charged me right away. I went into panic mode and called them immediately. They told me I had made an advance purchase and it was nonrefundable. Fear struck me as I realized that was my rent money! I tried to explain my situation to the woman on the phone, and she tried to transfer me to a manager, who had already gone home for the day.

I sent a silent prayer up to God, begging him for help. God was giving me a sense of peace as I prayed. In the end, the very kind front desk clerk called the manager for me, and not only did the hotel refund my money, they also saved our reservation. After I hung up the phone, I hit the ground with tears in my eyes and thanked God for his help in time of need.

Our God is a God that can change people's hearts, fix any problem, and provide for any need. When you ask Jesus to come into your heart and accept him as your personal Savior, you become a part of God's family, and he always takes care of his children. He cares about everything that bothers us, no matter how big or how small the matter might be.

Remember the next time you hit panic mode that there is an Almighty God that you can turn to for help.

"For whosoever shall call upon the name of the Lord shall be saved" (Romans 10:13).

"The Lord is nigh unto all them that call upon him, to all that call upon him in truth" (Psalm 145:18).

"In my distress I called upon the Lord, and cried unto my God: he heard my voice out of his temple, and my cry came before him, even into his ears" (Psalm 18:6).

"Trust ye in the LORD for ever: for in the LORD JEHOVAH is everlasting strength" (Isaiah 26:4).

RUN THE RACE

It was the day of the Celebrate Pink 5K race for breast cancer awareness, my first road race ever. I was so excited! Even though I was sick with a head cold and it was a little chilly out, I was determined to run this race. So I filled my pockets with tissues and headed out. The race was tough with feeling sick to my stomach and blowing my nose every ten minutes, but I didn't do too badly after all. It helped to have three of my running buddies cheering me on and running with me.

It turned out to be a beautiful day in Portsmouth. I was praying all the way through as well as reciting my life verse, "I can do all things through Christ which strengtheneth me" (Phil. 4:13). I also sang some hymns in my head. I was going to finish strong. At the end, I burst into a sprint to cross the finish line!

The race reminded me so much of running the race of life. That morning I read my Bible before I headed out and found a verse in Hebrews that talked about "running the race set before us."[24] It mentioned sin getting in our way and having witnesses watching us.

Just like there are people watching you in a 5K race, there are always people watching you in life. We see family, friends, and church members cheering us on, but there are also silent witnesses we don't realize are there. Are we not to make sure we run a steady course in front of them?

They see our behaviors and our reactions to the things we go through in life. Oh, we must beware of that nasty sin that gets in our way. It can be something as simple as getting angry at another person. Our witnesses see that. We have to try to perform the best we can and remember that what goes on in our hearts is reflected on the outside of us.

Hebrews 12:2 talked about focusing on Jesus. He ran his race here on earth for us. He put up with the shame and the way people treated him. He bore our sins

---

[24] "Wherefore seeing we also are compassed about with so great a cloud of witnesses, let us lay aside every weight, and the sin which doeth so easily beset us, and let us run with patience the race that is set before us, Looking unto Jesus the author and finisher of our faith; who for the joy that was set before him endured the cross, despising the shame, and is set down at the right hand of the throne of God" (Heb. 12:1).

so we could meet him in heaven one day as he sits at the right hand of the Father, making intersession for us.

Keep in mind all he did when he ran his race. We are to keep our focus on him as we overcome all the obstacles before us. So run your race today with confidence! Run your race for Jesus!

"I have fought a good fight, I have finished my course, I have kept the faith: Henceforth there is laid up for me a crown of righteousness, which the Lord, the righteous judge, shall give me at that day: and not to me only, but unto all them also that love his appearing" (2 Timothy 4:7–8).

"Know ye not that they which run in a race run all, but one receiveth the prize? So run, that ye may obtain" (I Corinthians 9:24)

STAND LIKE THE EVERGREEN

Disappointment often brings anger and sadness with it. It was so hard driving the empty bus back to the school. I had just dropped off a group of high school students for their theater competition. My son was supposed to be performing with them. He was struck down with a bad case of the flu and had to stay home. My heart was breaking for him.

As I was driving, I noticed the many trees on the side of the road that were barren of leaves. It was then that the beautiful-looking pine trees caught my eye. There they were, so perfectly shaped with their branches full of lush green needles.

They often go unnoticed during the summer months when all the other trees are full of leaves. No matter what, they continue to stand tall. Even when the cold weather sets in, those evergreen trees are still full and green. In the worst winter storms, they still stand, raising their branches and pointing up to heaven as if they are praising God through it all.

Oh, if we could only be that strong and full of faith when the hard times come our way. The Bible tells us we can. The evergreen cannot stand on its own. It needs the strength of its mighty Creator. We too need our faith and strength to come from God. He is our sure foundation, the solid rock we stand on in time of need.

Life may bring us disappointments, but God will give us a silver lining in every cloud. He is our blessed hope. Our everlasting redeemer and his Word promises that "all things work together for good to them that love God, to them who are the called according to his purpose" (Rom. 8:28).

Whatever we may lack, whether it be food, shelter, or faith, all we need to do is ask him, and he will always provide for our needs.

"O come, let us sing unto the Lord: let us make a joyful noise to the rock of our salvation" (Psalm 95:1).

"I will say of the Lord, He is my refuge and my fortress: my God; in him will I trust" (Psalm 91:2).

"And Moses said unto the people, Fear ye not, stand still, and see the salvation of the LORD, which he will shew to you to day" (Exodus 14:13).

"What time I am afraid, I will trust in thee" (Psalm 56:3).

SURVIVING THE STORMS

God did not promise once you became a Christian that you would avoid storms in life. He actually warned us in the Bible that there would be trials and tribulations. The only difference is, as a Christian, you will be better equipped to survive the storms when they come.

In the book of Acts, the apostle Paul was on a ship heading toward Rome when it was caught in a euroclydon, a violent storm like a hurricane. Paul was surprisingly calm during the storm. He encouraged the other people on the ship to not be afraid. He even told them to take time to eat and gain their strength. God had assured Paul that he would arrive in Rome and all 276 people would survive as well.

I am sure the people hearing this had hope they would sail through the storm right to Rome. But God had other plans. He had a special mission for Paul to complete first. They ended up shipwrecked on an island, where Paul was able to be a Christian witness and help the so-called barbarous people living there. The indigenous tribe ended up showing nothing but kindness to their visitors from the moment they arrived.

Anyone in this situation would have lost hope and been scared to death. Not Paul. He had great faith and trusted in the one true living God. He knew God would protect him no matter what. He knew God would always keep his word. Even when a poisonous snake bit Paul while he was putting some wood on the fire, he still remained calm, shook it off, and walked away unharmed.

Imagine being able to handle whatever life throws your way with that kind of peace and confidence knowing you will get through it all. True peace doesn't happen when it's calm. It happens when the storms are going on around you, but you feel calm and safe inside. God will always restore hope in our hearts when we need it most.

I love the saying, "Keep your eyes on the horizon." I know over on that horizon there is something far greater than this life has to offer. There is a promise of eternal life in heaven. And the way there is by trusting Jesus as your personal Savior so he can safely carry you through the storms until you reach your glorified home in heaven.

"And the night following the Lord stood by him, and said, Be of good cheer, Paul: for as thou hast testified of me in Jerusalem, so must thou bear witness also at Rome" (Acts 23:11).

"These things I have spoken unto you, that in me ye might have peace. In the world ye shall have tribulation: but be of good cheer; I have overcome the world" (John 16:33).

"And I give unto them eternal life; and they shall never perish, neither shall any man pluck them out of my hand" (John 10:28).

"Be strong and of a good courage, fear not, nor be afraid of them: for the LORD thy God, he it is that doth go with thee; he will not fail thee, nor forsake thee" (Deuteronomy 31:6).

THE MIGHTY OAK

God uses examples in nature to teach us about life. Each individual creature or flower he created gives us a lesson we can reflect on and learn from.

As I gaze out my window, I see the mighty oak tree standing tall on a cold January day. I remember hearing how oak trees don't lose their leaves until spring. It's almost like they refuse to let go of what they have. They cling to their leaves for as long as they can even though the leaves are already dead. They don't want to lose all their leaves and become bare like the other trees around them. They're afraid of letting go and standing empty in the cold.

Come spring, the other trees sprout new green buds, the promises of hope and new growth. They are rewarded for their faith and trust in God and given new signs of a better life. The oak trees are suddenly jealous and quickly try to shed their old leaves so they too can sprout new buds.

Imagine if they were as trusting as the trees around them. They wouldn't be late in joining in the celebration of spring. They would be rejoicing along with the rest of nature.

Are you finding yourself to be as the mighty oak? Are there things in your life that you refuse to let go of even though they serve no purpose in your life? Fear not, dear one. Let go and shed your leaves. There is always a promise of spring with the Lord Jesus. He never fails to bring us through the cold winters. Don't lose hope, and don't be afraid to be left bare and empty. For it is only when we let go and shed our past, our pride, and our sins that Jesus can give us something new and more beautiful. When we trust him as our Savior and Lord, we too can look forward to the great celebration of eternal spring in heaven, a spring celebration that will never end.

"For there is hope of a tree, if it be cut down, that it will sprout again, and that the tender branch thereof will not cease" (Job 14:7).

"Verily, verily, I say unto you, Except a corn of wheat fall into the ground and die, it abideth alone: but if it die, it bringeth forth much fruit" (John 12:24).

"Brethren, I count not myself to have apprehended: but this one thing I do, forgetting those things which are behind, and reaching forth unto those things which are before, I press toward the mark for the prize of the high calling of God in Christ Jesus" (Philippians 3:13–14).

"Be of good courage, and he shall strengthen your heart, all ye that hope in the Lord" (Psalm 31:24).

WHAT ARE YOU WAITING FOR?

Waiting is a part of life—waiting in line at the store, waiting at the traffic light, waiting for the next blessing, waiting to overcome the next challenge, and waiting for the next exciting thing to happen, the next season, or next vacation. There's even waiting to get better when you're sick. Lately I have been waiting for God to reveal to me his plan for my life.

If we spend all of our time always waiting, we tend to miss out on the joy and blessings that are happening right now. Our attitude changes for the worse, and all our waiting turns into impatience and then frustration, and all that leads to nothing but stress.

I say no more waiting. Let's not wait anymore. I just want to be. I want to stop in the moment I'm in right now and be content. It's time to wait upon the Lord. When we wait upon the Lord, we aren't really waiting but resting. We're still and at peace as God is accomplishing things for us.

If we wait on the Lord, we will have courage and the strength and hope we need to get through the trials we face in life. He alone can heal us, provide for us, and solve our problems. We just need to trust him.

I have decided to stop waiting for the things of this world and wait upon Jesus. Let me ask you, "What are you waiting for?"

"Wait on the LORD: be of good courage, and he shall strengthen thine heart: wait I say, on the LORD" (Psalm 27:14).

"But they that wait upon the LORD shall renew their strength; they shall mount up with wings as eagles; they shall run, and not be weary; and they shall walk, and not faint" (Isaiah 40:31).

"For the LORD God is a sun and shield: the LORD will give grace and glory: no good thing will he withhold from them that walk uprightly. O LORD of hosts, blessed is the man that trusteth in thee" (Psalm 84:11–12).

"The God of my rock; in him will I trust: he is my shield, and the horn of my salvation, my high tower, and my refuge, my savior" (2 Samuel 22:3).

WHAT'S HOLDING YOU BACK?

Picture yourself running in a race. You run as hard as you can, but you just can't seem to get to the finish line. Something keeps getting in your way. It's an obstacle that you have tried to overcome before, but no matter how hard you try, it keeps holding you back. Now picture yourself stopping for a moment to pray. You close your eyes, and when you open them, your obstacle is not only gone, but you're at the finish line, and you've won the race.

Now imagine that this isn't a race but your very own life. What obstacles are keeping you from accomplishing your dreams or preventing you from getting to where you want to be?

I heard in a message once that the number-one person holding you back from accomplishing your goals is yourself. Emotionally, we let things get in our way, and then we stumble and fall. It all starts with our heart. There are obstacles in life that can keep our faith from growing and keep us from becoming all that God wants us to be.

Forgiveness: Not only does forgiveness free the person you forgive, it also sets you free as well. If there is someone you need to forgive but can't because you are holding onto a grudge, just know it will keep you bound emotionally and spiritually. It can even make you physically ill. That is one obstacle that will hurt you more than it will others.

Holding onto the past: I know from experience that there is one person who is really hard to forgive. That person, believe it or not, is yourself. I learned how to forgive people by watching my mother. She really trusted God to help her forgive those that hurt her. For some reason though, she found it hard to forgive herself for the mistakes and bad choices she made in her past.

I too have held onto guilt and heartache from the sins of my past. Whether we keep reliving the behaviors we once had or the devil keeps reminding us of what we've done, our own wrongdoings seem to stay with us no matter how hard we try to run away from them.

Feeling loss: Even if you're a Christian, losing someone you love in your life still takes a lot out of you. You hurt emotionally, spiritually, and physically. As time passes, some people heal with grace, but others will strive to keep the person *alive* in their mind for as long as they can. Even if they believe their loved one is in heaven, they just can't let them go.

Losing someone you love doesn't always come by death. We can lose people by painful breakups, divorce, friendships ending, or family members fighting. Whatever the source of your loss, holding on to the sorrow you feel can hold you back from healing and moving on.

Whatever the obstacles are in your life, you may find it's impossible to overcome them on your own. Maybe it's time you reach out to someone who can take your burdens for you and set you free, one who can heal your heart and bring you the peace you've been longing for.

I know just the person you need. A hymn says, "Burdens are lifted at Calvary; Jesus is very near."[25] I have found the greatest strength you can have in life comes when you surrender. Just like you pictured yourself in the race I described above, take time to stop for a moment and pray. Ask Jesus to come into your heart and give you the strength and healing you need to surrender your burdens to him and set you free. You will be surprised to see how he can help you overcome any obstacle in your way and get you to that finish line to win the race.

"The thief cometh not, but for to steal, and to kill, and to destroy: I am come that they might have life, and that they might have it more abundantly" (John 10:10).

"He healeth the broken in heart, and bindeth up their wounds" (Psalm 147:3).

"Take my yoke upon you, and learn of me; for I am meek and lowly in heart: and ye shall find rest unto your souls" (Matthew 11:29).

"Peace I leave with you, my peace I give unto you: not as the world giveth, give I unto you. Let not your heart be troubled, neither let it be afraid" (John 14:27).

---

[25] John M. Moore, "Burdens Are Lifted at Calvary," http://revivalsounds.homestead.com/midihymnhistory/burdensareliftedatcalvary.html.

WOULD YOU GIVE YOUR ALL?

Think of something that means a lot to you—a personal possession, a career, or a beloved person. If God asked you to surrender that something over to him and walk away from it, would you?

That is something I had to do recently with the summer camp job I love. It is the first job that makes me feel like I can't wait to be there. Even with the long hours of planning and the days where it seems like the kids aren't listening and things don't go according to plan, it is still my favorite job. I gladly arrive early and leave late feeling grateful to be there.

This coming week, my schedule was knocked down to two days because a low number of kids was in my group. I wish I could say I handled the news with a godly attitude. Nope, I crashed emotionally. Angry and upset, I just burst into tears. I asked God, "Why?" Then I went into panic mode as I realized there was no way I would survive financially this month.

It wasn't until I was preparing my Sunday school lesson that I saw that God was trying to teach me something. The lesson was about Abraham when God asked him to sacrifice his promised son, Isaac. Abraham didn't hesitate. He immediately obeyed God and surrendered his son to him. Before that event took place, Abraham was asked years earlier to trust God and leave his home, his family, and all he knew to wander in the desert to an unknown place.

I thought to myself, *How can anyone do that?* God so wisely brought to mind the missionaries we support at my church. God answered me with, "How do they do it?" Missionaries all over the world give up the life they know and give their all to God. They leave behind their careers, homes, and families to travel to an unfamiliar destination. Some of them even bring their children with them, not knowing how they will provide for them. They sacrifice all they have and love to live by faith, putting their full trust in the Lord. Amazingly enough, they are the happiest and calmest people I have ever met in my life. It is only by God's grace and love that they can accomplish this.

Missionaries know that this life isn't the only life to live for. They are storing up treasures in heaven while spending their time telling others about the precious gift of salvation Jesus has to offer.

Perhaps God is asking me to be willing to sacrifice the job I love so I can spend some time serving him. He may want me to start working on that book I have been wanting to write. Whatever the reason may be, I know I need to be willing to give my all to him.

"He saith unto him the third time, Simon, son of Jonas, lovest thou me? Peter was grieved because he said unto him the third time, Lovest thou me? And he said unto him, Lord, thou knowest all things; thou knowest that I love thee. Jesus saith unto him, Feed my sheep" (John 21:17).

"But lay up for yourselves treasures in heaven, where neither moth nor rust doth corrupt, and where thieves do not break through nor steal: For where your treasure is, there will your heart be also" (Matthew 6:20–21).

"Then Jesus beholding him loved him, and said unto him, One thing thou lackest: go thy way, sell whatsoever thou hast, and give to the poor, and thou shalt have treasure in heaven: and come, take up the cross, and follow me" (Mark 10:21).

YOU ARE VALUABLE

eBay is something we are all familiar with. It has helped many people clean out the clutter in their homes and earn a little extra cash. My son was on eBay one day when he suddenly called out to me. He was so happy to find out he had the same small Darth Vader Lego figure that was going for $120. He immediately put it up for sale. I asked him to look up the value of some animal figurines, and he said they were only worth about twenty dollars.

Earlier that day, we were at the mall, and I happened to pick up a shirt that caught my eye. I was shocked to see it cost fifty dollars. I carefully put it back and walked out the door, saying to myself, "Savers, here I come."

It amazes me the value we place on certain earthly things. You can have two purses that look alike, but one is worth seventy dollars and the other only fifteen dollars because of who made them.

Aren't you glad we have a loving Savior who doesn't see things the way we do? A homeless man on the street is just as precious to him as a prince in a palace. Jesus loved us before we even knew who he was. He saw us as something worthy to pursue. He knows how much we need him in our lives. He reaches down to pick us up and draw us to him. He holds us close in his loving embrace and whispers ever so softly to tell us, "You were worth every suffering moment I endured on the cross."

It doesn't matter who we are or what our life has been like. We will always be valuable in God's eyes. It is only when we try to get to know him more that we see how much he truly loves us. Then we know how truly valuable and precious his gift of salvation is to us.

In the loving hands of God, you will always be of great value.

"Before I formed thee in the belly I knew thee; and before thou camest forth out of the womb I sanctified thee, and I ordained thee a prophet unto the nations" (Jeremiah 1:5).

"Are not two sparrows sold for a farthing? And one of them shall not fall on the ground without your Father. But the very hairs of your heard are all numbered. Fear ye not therefore, ye are of more value than many sparrows" (Matthew 10:29–31).

"Forasmuch as ye know that ye were not redeemed with corruptible things, as silver and gold, from your vain conversation received by tradition from your fathers; But with the precious blood of Christ, as of a lamb without blemish and without spot" (1 Peter 1:18–19).

PERSONAL INVITATION

You're invited! A great celebration is waiting for you, one with a great feast and people from all over the world. No one will ever go hungry or be sad. There will be no more wars but a peace that lasts for all eternity. Joy will be springing up in your heart continually. You will forever be in the loving arms of Jesus, the one who died to make you free. Your clothes will never wear out and always be in fashion. You will be comfortably clothed in righteousness. You will forever have a home in heaven. Are you ready? Are you excited to come?

You will need just one thing, a personal invitation from the Lord and Savior, Jesus Christ. Guess what? He has that invitation all ready and waiting for you to accept it. His invitation is for you to know him and accept him as your Savior and Redeemer. Do you know Jesus personally? Would you like to? He is just one prayer away.

Lord Jesus, I admit I am a sinner. I know you died on the cross to pay for my sins. I invite you to come into my heart and accept you as my personal Savior. In Jesus's name I pray, Amen.

Printed in the United States
By Bookmasters